Nailed It!

Quetzal Mama's Toolkit for Extraordinary College Essays

ROXANNE OCAMPO

ISBN- 13-978-1502390028

ISBN- 10- 1502390027

Edited by Margarita Maestas

Cover design by Milagro Marketing

Cover illustration by Will Orozco

Student Photos by Estrada Photography

About the Author Photo by Cisco Kidd Photography

Dedication

This book is dedicated to two inspirational scholars
who exemplify the Quetzal Mama[TM] mission:

Alexis Velasquez Reynoso
Sophomore, Merrill F. West High School

&

Hector Olmedo
Sophomore, Tracy High School

Alexis & Hector — stay on your path toward academic excellence.
We are counting on you to make a profound contribution to our world.

Table of Contents

Part One
Overview of the College Application Essay

Part Two
The Mechanics of the Personal Statement

Acknowledgments

The reason you are reading this book is the direct result of extraordinary contributions from extraordinary individuals. Nearly all of the assistance required to produce this book was donated, in one form or another, by generous individuals. In many cases, I had never met these individuals in person. They volunteered their time or expertise simply with the hope that their contribution would help Latino youth achieve their dream of college admission. Whether it was a monetary gift, the gift of time, loaned expertise or mentorship, or simply the gift of encouragement, the effects of these gifts appear on the next 200 plus pages.

Some may view these gifts as purely "luck," while others may call it "karma." Still, others may refer to these gifts as "blessings." Regardless of how we may wish to interpret these gifts, the outpouring of support convinces me that the spirit of community stewardship is alive and well. For this reason, I have so many people to thank.

The Quetzal Mama students who opened their hearts and shared their stories — thank you for your generosity in sharing your work so others can become successful in their quest for college.

Arturo Ocampo, My Husband—I am extremely grateful for your continued support throughout the writing of this book, as well as assisting me with workshops, logistical aspects, and encouraging me to go forward.

Carlos, Gabi, and Emilio, My Children—I appreciate how you listen, enthusiastically, to all of my schemes, themes, and dreams. You are my Latino Superstars, and I am extremely proud to be your Quetzal Mama.

Margarita Maestas, My Editor—Thank you for jumping into round two, and generously sharing your extraordinary talents! You are *marvelous*! Your gifts are truly a blessing.

Milagro Marketing—Especially David Ocampo, Sergio Estrada, and the artwork of artist, Will Orozco. I am grateful for your time, patience, and generosity in artfully capturing the essence of the Quetzal Mama spirit on the cover of the book. I knew you'd nail it!

Ruben Navarrette, Jr., — You "nailed" the Foreword! It is truly an honor to highlight the inspiring words of a nationally syndicated, *Latino* columnist. I couldn't have asked for more.

Estrada Photos —Especially Sergio Estrada. The time and care you took in capturing the student's images for this book is clearly evident. Your work is stellar!

Martin Mares, My Friend—Without your "Ninja Networking" skills, I would not have been able to network with influential persons to extend my publishing reach. Your generosity and mentorship are cherished.

The Aztlan Car Club & Los Viejitos Car Club—Especially Tony Gasca, Ernie Juarez, and Cisco Garcia. Your generous spirit and dedication to serve our Latino youth is commendable. You "nailed" the "About the Author" photo!

Dr. Angélica Pérez-Litwin—*Gracias* for taking time out of your busy schedule to read the manuscript and provide an excellent endorsement for the back cover.

Stephanie Bravo — I am so appreciative of your gift of time and genuine interest to read the manuscript and provide your endorsement for the back cover. *Gracias!*

The Quetzal Mama Focus Group—The following individuals volunteered their time and energies in reading my manuscript, offering suggestions, and giving me encouragement and support at the initial stages of this book. I am grateful to this extraordinary team! In alphabetical order:

Cynthia Arellano, AVID Teacher Poway Unified
Elisavet Barajas, Math Teacher/Coach, Tracy Unified
Minerva Gonzalez, CAMP Director, CSU San Marcos
Anne Green, Dir. Secondary Education, Vista Unified
Roberta Hernandez, Oakdale Unified
Julie Johnson, Director GEAR UP Mira Costa College
Gabriela Kovuts-Murillo, Director Barrio Logan College Institute
Martin Mares, CEO Ivy League Project
Andres Martin, Counselor, Ramona Unified
Dr. Arturo Ocampo, Assoc. Vice President, CSUSM
Crystal Ortiz, Counselor, San Marcos High School
Cecilia Rocha, Director GEAR UP Palomar College
David Varela, President, Reaching for the Stars Foundation

Focus Group Team: High School & College Students
Gabriela Acevedo, Delta College
Alexis Buz, UC San Diego
Vanessa Fregoso, UCLA
Rosabelle Hernandez, Oakdale High School
Gabriella Herrera, Harvard
Carlos Ocampo, UC Santa Cruz
Rodrigo Tellez, UC Berkeley

Focus Group Team: The 2014/2015 Quetzal Mama Scholars

Jorge Angón

Karen Barragan

Andrea Carreno

Erina Chavez

Chelsea Flores

Cassandra Galiza

Yadira Garcia

Natalie Gonzalez

Diana Hernandez

José Hurtado

Jonathan Mendez

Maria Montero

Josue Morales

Tabita Quiñones

Sandra Ramos

Stephanie Sanchez

About the Author

Roxanne Ocampo is a proud Latina mom and author of *Nailed It! Quetzal Mama's Toolkit for Extraordinary College Essays.*" She is also the author of the popular book, "*Flight of the Quetzal Mama: How to Raise Latino Superstars and Get Them into the Best Colleges*" (Available *en Español*). She is the CEO of Quetzal Mama™ – a college admission coaching practice for Latino students. She runs Quetzal Mama Scholars, a seven month, intensive college admissions program for students attending school districts in North San Diego County. Additionally, she conducts workshops and boot camps throughout the U.S. focused on college admission strategies. Her workshops cover K-5, middle school, and high school strategies for college admission and competitive scholarships. The students from her practice have earned admission to the most prestigious universities as well as national scholarship awards.

She is a Doctoral Fellow in Educational Leadership at the University of California at San Diego. Her Dissertation and research topic is *"Undermatching"* of low-income, first-generation, high performing, Latino students. She holds a Master's Degree and Bachelor's Degree in English from California State University East Bay. The theories and philosophy that guide her teaching and publications are situated in Critical Race Theory. Her coaching practice is founded on the principle of stewardship; providing free services for qualifying students and families. She was born and raised in the Bay Area (San Jose) and resides in San Marcos, California.

Her work has been featured on ABC News, Good Day Sacramento, and Sacramento & Co. She is a feature writer for regional and national magazines, and has coached thousands of students throughout the US.

Roxanne is married to Dr. Arturo E. Ocampo—a Civil Rights and Education Law Attorney, and Associate Vice President of Diversity & Educational Equity at CSU San Marcos. Together they have raised three incredible children following the 10 Quetzal Mama Principles: Carlos (UC Santa Cruz Class of 2015), Gabriella (Harvard Class of 2015), and Emilio (Cornell, "Future" Class of 2023).

Foreword

*I*t's been almost 30 years since I first walked through Dexter Gate and into Harvard Yard. Carved in stone overhead is the unofficial greeting of America's oldest university: *"Enter to Grow in Wisdom."* On the reverse side, visible as you're walking back through the same gate, comes a direct order: *"Depart to Serve Better Thy Country and Thy Kind."*

My friends and I are still trying to live up to that directive, and I expect we'll be trying for the rest of our days. It's a mission you never complete. On a grand scale, the idea of public service might impact the lives of millions of people in this country or around the world. But in our everyday lives, it might mean simply offering encouragement, a helping hand and the right tools to a new generation of bright and motivated students eager to venture out and enjoy some of the experiences that you have.

Like most graduates of prestigious universities, I have for many years been asked what it takes for young people to be among the six or seven students admitted to a school like Harvard from every 100 applicants who throw their hats in the ring. And, more recently, as someone who makes his living through the written word, I'm also often asked what makes for a good column, a good story, a good essay.

At the intersection of those two queries, you'll find what I believe to be the single most important factor in any application to an Ivy League school, or other private university: the application essay. Enough books have been written by current and former admissions officers over the years that we now understand the fundamentals of what it takes to be admitted to selective colleges: exemplary grades, high-level courses, demonstrated leadership ability, strong extracurricular activities, a solid interview, and a compelling essay that gives us a peek at the essence of the individual.

The reason I say that the essay is the most important piece of that puzzle is because — while there is little that a student can do in 11th or 12th grade to turn around a shoddy transcript or light coursework or a list of out-of-class activities that perhaps isn't as substantial as it could be — the essay has a redemptive quality. For admissions officers who might look at 100 applications a day, a good essay can jump off the page, grab the reader by the lapels, and demand to be noticed. Clearly, 500-700 words can't work miracles. Yet, a well-written college essay can tip the scales in favor of an applicant, who might not otherwise have been accepted. That is, if the student nails it!

That, appropriately, is the title of Roxanne Ocampo's new book. "Nailed It! Quetzal Mama's Toolkit for Extraordinary College Essays" spells out what it takes to write a successful application essay in clear but passionate language. A high-energy and high-achieving college admissions coach who is building a folkloric following as "Quetzal Mama" among aspiring college students of modest means and humble backgrounds, Ocampo lays out a recipe for good college essays. She does so with humor and flair, as when she describes the personal statement of an application as being "like a *taco de carne asada.*" Don't miss that chapter.

In these pages, you'll find helpful tips for writing a good essay that — allow with the other fundamentals of a strong application — might just improve your chances of getting into the college or university of your dreams. And they're all provided to you by someone who understands the value of dreams because she's living her own.

If you want to make *carne asada tacos*, you have to crack open this book. You get the ingredients, the spices, the guidance, the encouragement. Of course, cooking up the right essay is up to you. But, fear not. Quetzal Mama is by your side.

So what are you waiting for? Light the grill -- and get cooking."
— Ruben Navarrette, Jr.

Ruben Navarrette, Jr., is a USA Today Board of Contributors, nationally syndicated Columnist with The Washington Post, Weekly Commentator for CNN, Commentator on NPR's "Tell Me More with Michel Martin," and author of "A Darker Shade of Crimson: Odyssey of a Harvard Chicano."

Introduction

It is true — I have one of the most interesting and fascinating jobs in the world. It is interesting because I work with a diverse spectrum of Latino superstars throughout the United States. Some of these students are Ivy League "contenders" with near perfect GPA's, fifth to tenth percentile performance on SAT/ACT and AP exams, extensive extracurricular activities, and admirable leadership and community service. Another group of students are also college bound, pursuing admission to a wider range of selectivity within their college choices. And, yet, another group of students are community college superstars, pursuing transfer from a two-year college to a four-year college. Regardless of their aspirations, I have the honor and privilege of guiding these superstars at a critical point in their academic journey.

Although the students I serve represent a diverse spectrum, they share a similar educational journey. Their journey to college includes attending low resourced high schools — many without comprehensive AP or IB programs, lack of high school counselling services — many with a 800:1 counselor/student ratio, lack of tailored and individualized college-going information, lack of financial aid knowledge, ineffective high school intervention programs, anti-social messaging regarding intellectual or cultural inferiority, and lack of socio-cultural capital to navigate the college process. Adding to these challenges, the majority of these students are also low-income, first generation, English Language Learners, and many are undocumented.

As evidenced by these compounding factors, it is truly a miracle these superstars somehow arrived at my doorstep. However, while these superstars have admirably overcome significant hurdles along their pathway to college, they are often unprepared to confront an unforeseen challenge: the Personal Statement. So, each year during the hectic college admissions cycle, their draft essays land on my virtual desk. And, each year I identify the same patterns and trouble spots.

Regardless of gender, geography, or socioeconomic status, these superstars tend to struggle with the same concepts. They struggle to create a Personal Statement that reflects their intellectual curiosity, that showcases their unique talents and skills, and that provides the admission reader with insight into the distinct characteristics that will make them a fascinating addition to the incoming freshman class.

My quest, therefore, was to create a toolkit containing essential components to craft an exceptional college essay. In addition to essential components, I also wanted to include common mistakes made by high school students. Finally, I wanted to present a toolkit that would be meaningful for a broad spectrum of students — those students pursuing admission to a broad spectrum of college level selectivity.

Now, you would think with a title like, "Nailed It!" this book would be about the mechanics of writing an essay. It is not. My expectation is that students reading this book *already* know the basic mechanics of writing an essay: how to articulate a thesis, compose an introductory paragraph, supporting paragraphs, and a conclusion. This book is for those students who know how to write an essay, but are unsure how to select a particular theme, how to select an appropriate prompt, or how to market their profile effectively. This book was also written specifically for Latino students — with culturally-relevant strategies and methods designed to capture our unique life experiences and perspectives.

Although the purpose of this book is to help students with their Personal Statement for college admission, the tips and strategies in this book are also applicable in other contexts. Students can use these tools when responding to prompts for scholarships, internships, and other competitive programs.

All of the samples provided are from actual students I've coached over the years. These students gave me permission to use their name and photograph in the hopes that sharing their personal story will inspire or help other Latino students in their quest to gain admission to a selective university. In other cases, I intentionally used fictitious names, towns, and schools, to remove any potentially identifiable characteristics.

I also intentionally use humor in many of my examples and descriptions. My humor is not intended to downplay the significance of this part of the application process. Rather, it is intended to engage my readers and help them relax during this stressful process. Furthermore, I intentionally write in a "motherly" tone that "*keeps it real.*" I don't sugarcoat the content, or gently nudge students to consider a particular strategy. Instead, I rely on my "Quetzal Mama" persona, instructing students in a blunt, candid, straight-forward way.

Why I Wrote This Book?

I wrote this book for three reasons. First, I am passionate about helping marginalized students actualize their true potential. My

Doctoral research and Dissertation topic is "*Undermataching*." Put simply, *Undermatching* is a phenomenon where high performing students meet rigorous admissions standards for selective colleges, yet they either forego college altogether or enroll in a college significantly below their qualifications. This phenomenon disproportionately impacts low-income, historically underrepresented, first generation high school students. I wrote this book to help high-performing students mitigate one of the most important aspects of the college application process — the essay.

Second, selective college admissions is an elite business. Often, the exclusive inner workings of the admission process is reserved to those within a tight network — university presidents, chancellors, and admission executives. These high-level university executives define the mission and goals of their selection process. In turn, admission administrators and staff discretely design protocols, practices, and rubrics, to fastidiously adhere to the direction of the executives. Then, there is a sub-group of outsiders called "Admission Consultants" whose job is to interpret, decode, and devise strategies to help inform their "base." These high-end consultants earn a paycheck from their "base" who represent "high net-worth clients." This book is my way of sharing my specialized knowledge with *my base* — a group of students who cannot afford the services of a professional consultant.

The final reason I wrote this book was to produce a counter-narrative. The stories my students produce each year represent a narrative rarely publicized. This new narrative is a more accurate representation of the intellectual capital our Latino youth possess. Their narrative represents intellectual brilliance, an incredible work ethic, discipline, and strong sense of *familia*. This narrative counters the myths of "special" admission for "minority" candidates or the myth that Latino parents don't care about education. While reading the accounts of my students, you will hear the voice of disciplined, diligent, and determined students who are advancing—against all odds, toward selective university admission. And, you will hear the voice of their *familias* who supported them along their journey.

Why is This Book Needed?

From my research, an admissions reader will spend approximately two to three minutes reading an applicant's essay. In three minutes or less, how do you convince the admissions team you are the candidate they should admit? In this book you will learn how to select an appropriate prompt, how to effectively market your profile, how best to articulate your unique qualities, and how to avoid some common mistakes.

All things being equal, the Personal Statement is *the* factor that separates students being "considered" from those being "admitted." Don't be fooled. Remember I said, "All things being equal." A less than stellar academic profile with a wonderful essay will not get you accepted into a selective college. However, for academically strong students competing against other academically strong candidates, an effective essay might provide the edge.

The bottom line? This book is needed because there is no such thing as "luck" within the college admissions process. Luck has very little to do with it. "Luck" might occur if you are the one oboe player Dartmouth is seeking in a particular admission year. The truth is, luck cannot overcome an inferior essay that leaves the reader uninspired. While there are no guaranteed formulas to gain admission to a particular college, there are methods and strategies to increase the odds. This book is intended to increase a student's odds of admission by providing both the art and science of writing a Personal Statement.

How is This Book Different from Other Essay Books?

As I contemplated this book, I wondered how to craft an essay-writing book that would be especially helpful and meaningful for Latino students. Having read nearly all of the top-selling college admissions essay-writing books, it became clear the majority of students featured in these books do not represent the socioeconomic or ethnocultural profile of the students I coach. The top-selling books on college essays predominantly feature stories and experiences of middle to high income students, from privileged backgrounds, who do not belong to an historically underrepresented minority group.

After determining that a book containing culturally-relevant strategies would resonate with Latino students, I wondered how I could structure the content for the greatest appeal. Fortunately, this answer was handed to me on a Saturday afternoon in Parlier, California.

In 2012 I was invited to present an essay-writing workshop to an elite group of Latino students representing the Ivy League Project. The workshop would take place in a small, agricultural town of Parlier in the Fresno valley of California. Martin Mares – CEO of the Ivy League Project, and the Chief Education Officer of Parlier Unified School District, invited me to present to his 21st cohort of students. After my presentation concluded, Mr. Mares asked his students, "Who wants to be first to provide a *Positive Affirmation Statement*?" This is just one of the leadership techniques Mr. Mares teaches his Ivy League cohort each year. His students — all dressed in professional business suits — shared how they appreciated I did not spend an hour focusing on theory and principles, but instead provided clear technical points with culturally-relevant examples.

Therefore, when I wrote this book I followed the same principles I use in my workshops: briefly teach theories *and* give plenty of culturally-relevant examples. In providing frameworks such as *Los Huesos*, the *Ganas* Principle, the TIN CASA rubric, and "The Personal Statement is like a *Taco de Carne Asada*" it is my hope students will become engaged. If students are engaged, it is likely they will follow the strategies to produce a stronger essay worthy of admission to the college of their dreams.

Finally, I gathered input from strategically comprised Focus Groups. These groups included high school students, teachers, secondary counselors, and Directors of college preparation programs. From their feedback, I modified and edited portions of the book so that the content would be more meaningful and interesting.

I am delighted to share this book, and I look forward to hearing from students across the US who successfully implemented the tools in this book. If you have a success story, write to me at quetzalmama@gmail.com.

Thank you for allowing me the honor to present my tips and strategies. I want you to "Nail" your college application essay.

¡Hechale todas las ganas del mundo! Buena suerte.
—Quetzal Mama

Part One

Overview of the College Application Essay

1

How to Use this Book

I 've worked with thousands of high school students, so I get you. You want quick answers. This book was designed to give you quick answers. Each chapter is designed to be a "stand alone" resource. You don't have to read each chapter or the entire book to learn valuable strategies.

This book is designed to be as broad as possible — useful for novice *and* advanced writers. Novice writers may wish to read through several sections prior to beginning the writing process. Advanced writers may wish to scan through the Table of Contents to find the topic most helpful at their stage of the writing process.

My writing strategies are simple. Start with *Los Huesos* — the bones. Gather your bones to set up your outline. Then, add flesh to your bones by the methods outlined in *The Personal Statement is like a Taco de Carne Asada.* Third, after you've drafted your essay, use the *TIN CASA* rubric to review the contents of your essay. Finally, review Section 4: *Blunders to Avoid* to ensure your essay is blunder free. *¡Eso es todo!*

If you're really short on time, go straight to the last section of the book to read actual essays. These essays quickly demonstrate the quality of writing required for selective universities. You will know immediately where you may need help.

2

Overview of the Personal Statement

What is the college application essay (aka "Personal State-ment"), how is this essay used in college admissions, who reads it, and how is this statement unique to Latino stu-dents? Let's cover each of these points below.

What is the Personal Statement?

The Personal Statement is an essay required by most selective col-leges and universities. There are generally three types of college appli-cations that require an essay or Personal Statement, including:

(1) Private Colleges — typically utilizing the Common Application;
(2) Public Research Universities including "Research 1" univer-sities — utilizing their proprietary application for all cam-puses within their region or state; and
(3) Private Universities that do not use the Common Application.

Private Colleges — The Common Application is an online appli-cation used by more than 500 private universities and colleges in the US. A student completes one "common" application that can be sent to multiple universities. Currently the Common App requires one

3

650-word Personal Statement (and some campuses require additional supplemental essays).

Public Research Universities – These include, but are not limited, to institutions such as University of California, University of Texas, or University of Colorado. These campuses have their own application and essay requirements. As an example, University of California requires two Personal Statements, for a total of 1,000 words. See Chapter 3: *"Selecting the Right Prompt."*

Private Universities that do not use the Common Application – Finally, there are selective universities that use neither of the above and instead have their own application and essays. Some of these campuses include Georgetown, MIT, and Rutgers, to name a few.

The essay provides an opportunity to articulate to the admissions team why you are special. It gets the reader beyond your stats – GPA, class rank, ACT or SAT score. It allows the reader to know you personally, providing a glimpse into your unique life experiences, such as:

- Passion for a particular discipline (Biological Sciences, Journalism, Engineering, etc.);
- Factors that influenced your academic performance respective to your high school campus;
- An appreciation for your cultural authenticity/ diversity;
- Obstacles you have overcome along your academic journey;
- All of the special details that help admissions folks learn about your unique characteristics and attributes – the

particular skills, strengths, and disposition that separate you from other candidates.

The above description is fairly generic, similar to what you might find if you Google "Personal Statements." This information is helpful, but does not tell you how to devise a winning Personal Statement. Keep reading.

How is it Used?

Before we talk about how your essay will be used, we need to talk about your application. Admissions teams will be evaluating your application on three dimensions.

First, they will assess your academic accomplishments. This can be easily discerned by your transcript and statistical data listed on your application. This includes your GPA, class rank, and performance on standardized college exams such as the SAT/ACT, SAT Subject Tests, and AP or IB Exam scores.

Second, they will review your extracurricular activities. This will also be discerned through your application by listing the various on-campus clubs, sports, and leadership activities, as well as your outside volunteer and community service activities.

Lastly, they will consider your personal qualities and character. This factor is a little tricky because your qualities and character cannot be objectively discerned through a list of activities or statistical analysis.

For this reason, selective universities use a "holistic" approach or "comprehensive review" in screening applicants. This means your *entire* student profile will be considered — both your unique background and academic statistics.

While the admissions reader may assume certain qualities and characteristics by reviewing your application, the best way to tell your story is through the Personal Statement. From reading about your personal traits and experiences, the admissions team carefully screens your statement to determine whether or not you will be a complimentary addition to their entering freshman class. This is a helpful bit of information, but it still will not help you devise a winning Personal Statement. Keep reading.

Who Reads It?

In addition to the Admissions staff, additional readers will likely review your essay including faculty within your discipline; college admission consultants; alumni; and in some cases, contracted essay readers unaffiliated with the university. These experienced essay readers will plow through each essay, evaluating and scoring *in three minutes or less*. During the admissions recruitment cycle, readers will read essays all day, for months at a time.

Hmm. This information is getting a bit more interesting. These combined tidbits are useful in helping you understand the Personal Statement. However, they still do not get to the main point. Keep reading.

How is this Statement Unique to Latino Students?

Based on my experience, culturally authentic Latino students and/ or first generation, low-income, historically underrepresented students have an edge when it comes to writing the Personal Statement. No, this doesn't mean "minority" students are assessed with "special" criteria (aka lower academic standards) than their non-minority peers. *This is a myth.* Let's be clear. Selective colleges have a general academic benchmark that students must meet to be considered for admission, period. However, once students have met that benchmark, they have an opportunity to shine within their Personal Statement.

To understand how race/ethnicity and socioeconomic status play a significant role in the evaluation of candidates for admission, consider the following two candidates:

Candidate A is a Latina student from Delano, California — an agricultural town ranked as one of the top three poorest regions in California. She will be the first in her family to attend college. She holds a 3.95 GPA, 1895 composite SAT score, and attends a low-resourced high school where the student to counselor ratio is 750:1. Her Personal Statement reflects how she is a surrogate parent for her four younger siblings so that her single-parent mother can work a graveyard shift. She has performed more than 400 hours of community service, tutoring migrant education students in math and science. Her life objective is to become a Legal Aid attorney in California to assist low-income residents with housing and employment rights.

7

Candidate B is a student from the affluent Menlo-Atherton suburb of Northern California, and attends an exclusive boarding school staffed with traditional counselors *and* college advisors. Both of her parents hold graduate degrees from Ivy League institutions. Since her freshman year in high school she has travelled each summer to various countries in Europe, Asia, and Africa. She holds a 3.60 GPA, and a composite SAT score of 1980. Her goal is to study journalism so that she can become a food blogger. Her Personal Statement reflects how her world view is influenced through summer vacations, eating interesting foods, and visiting museums throughout the world.

Which profile has the potential to be *most impactful* through a Personal Statement? Do we care that the composite SAT scores differ only by 85 points? What about the difference in GPA? Does the student's social and cultural capital influence the way an admissions reader views them?

While it is impossible to accurately predict the admission outcomes for these two students, we can anticipate that admissions officers would pay special attention to Candidate A. Why? This is because the academic merit of Candidate A is most impressive when you consider the obstacles she has overcome. Whereas, Candidate B's accomplishments are of no surprise. We fully expect that Candidate B should boast an impressive academic profile based on the privileges she has been afforded.

Candidate A indicates she will make use of every opportunity for intellectual growth. She would be an interesting addition to a future campus because of her unique life experiences. The academic gains she has made while situated in a low-resourced school and community, demonstrate she has the *ganas* to succeed in a rigorous academic program.

For these reasons, Candidate A's presence would *greatly benefit* any given entering freshman class. The benefit comes from what Candidate A offers: a high-performing student with a unique perspective, life experiences, and voice that would add to the diversity of their campus.

Hopefully, you can see that Candidate A has a distinct advantage *if* she writes a compelling essay. While the admissions representative may be familiar with Candidate A's school district, and can easily view extracurricular activities listed on the candidate's application, the representative cannot know the special circumstances and experiences impacting the student's journey to college. The representative won't know that Candidate A performed as a surrogate parent, was raised by a single mother working a graveyard shift, or how her experiences working with migrant youth and families influenced her decision to study law. These extra details that convey personal qualities and experiences will only emerge through a strong essay.

In the next chapters, you will learn how cultural authenticity and/or your membership in the demographic above, as evidenced through your writing, may provide a distinctive edge. Ah, here is a unique point for students. Now we are near the point where it all comes together and you learn the bottom line when it comes to the Personal Statement. Read on.

The Bottom Line

If you read my first book, *"Flight of the Quetzal Mama: How to Raise Latino Superstars and Get Them Into the Best Colleges"* you learned my theory about selective college admissions. Below is an excerpt where I discuss the bottom line of college admissions:

Selective colleges do not admit students because they "like" them. Most competitive colleges admit students who have convinced them that they are *the* student who will make a difference in the world, who will yield them a great return on their investment, and who will ultimately maintain their elite status. Their business is a continuous wheel, churning out the future leaders of our world who will eventually become the next cycle of alumni donors.

I'm not a pessimist, really. I'm just a reasonable person who appreciates the correlation between selective universities and the business world. What does this business model have to do with your Personal Statement? It means you have to figure out how to convince an admissions reader you are worthy of admission, that you are *the* student who will make a difference in the world, that you will make a great addition to their entering freshman class, and that you are *the* student who will yield them a strong return on their investment.

Now consider the old sage, *the best predictor of the future is the past.* Admissions readers will be looking at what you have done in the past and assume you will continue these behaviors in the future. They look at patterns of behavior when making an overall assessment of your profile. You must convince the reader you have the talent, skill, and personal disposition to get the job done. In other words, you must convince the reader that you have *ganas.* Let me repeat this important concept:

You Must Convince the Reader You Have *Ganas.*

How does *ganas* factor into your essay? *Ganas* is that non-tangible essence I want you to capture and convey to the admissions reader. This is where you bring it home. This book focuses on the *Ganas Principle*, and it is a critical tool to write an impressive Personal Statement. You will learn about *Ganas* in Part Three, Chapter 6 "The *Ganas* Principle."

Recap
Nearly all selective colleges require an essay.
The team of readers have various backgrounds.
Your essay is read in two-to-three minutes.
Applications are reviewed "holistically."
Three criteria: academic, extracurricular, and personal.
The Essay conveys personal characteristics and qualities.
Your goal is to convey *Ganas*.

3

Getting Started - the Logistics

opefully you are reading this section *long before* you begin writing your college application essay. Before you contemplate crafting your Personal Statement, you need some quick pointers.

Timing: Waiting Until the Last Minute

Boy, if I had a nickel for every student who came to me at the last minute and said, *"I'm stuck."* The reality is many students procrastinate because they do not appreciate one of the most critical components of the college application. Other students do not feel confident in their writing abilities; therefore, they procrastinate until the last minute. These students are paralyzed with anxiety and cannot seem to begin the writing process.

I still recall a student (I'll call him Adrian) who appeared at my doorstep at 9:00 p.m. on the evening that applications were due for all University of California campuses. It was November 30, 2010. With no time to spare, we sat down and quickly assessed his strengths and extracted his unique "selling points." I coached him in producing a winning essay. This student submitted his application just before midnight that same evening and, subsequently, received a full scholarship to a University of California campus.

Adrian's example is not typical. He had an admissions expert coaching him! Waiting until the last minute will yield a poor-quality essay that conveys: (a) you do not really care about your college application and, therefore, must not be serious about college; and (b) your writing quality is poor and, therefore, not representative of the quality of student they seek for admission. Neither of these scenarios is a viable option for you.

Everything Piles up at the Same Time!

High school seniors do not anticipate the huge pile-up of activities that occur in the fall during the college application season. It comes as a surprise, and they are often caught off guard. So, let me share with you what happens during this crazy time and why you shouldn't wait until the last minute to compose your essay:

First, most college applications are due around the same time. If you are applying Early Action, you are working with a November 1 deadline. Less than a month later, a *new* set of essays are due to institutions like the University of California. Since the essay prompts for private colleges and public universities are dissimilar, that means you are attempting to write several exceptional essays within a 30-day period.

Second, this time also coincides with the dates when many students schedule their SAT exams: early October and early December. This is also the "final stretch" for most students because they are trying to pull the highest GPA possible. All-nighters are the norm.

Third, if you are applying to multiple colleges via the Common Application, then in addition to the 650-word main essay, you may also be writing supplemental essays for some selective campuses (See Chapter 13 "Supplemental Essays"). Compounding the issue, what if you are applying to campuses that do not use the Common Application — like Georgetown, MIT, or Rutgers? Yep, you got it. More essays!

Let's break this down mathematically, to illustrate what this means. We will imagine you are applying to the following three schools, all of which have their own essay requirements:

Georgetown — Three essays required, at approximately 500 words each.
Stanford — One essay on the Common App at 650 words, plus three supplemental essays at 250 words each.
UC Berkeley — two essays, at approximately 500 words each (1000 total)

Yup, that's nine different essays. Yikes — that means your hand will be very tired typing 3,900 words in a very short time. Get my point? Don't even think about recycling previously written essays to meet your deadlines! We call this type of recycling, "re-purposing" and we will discuss the pitfalls of repurposing later in this chapter.

A fourth reason you shouldn't procrastinate is because you'll need to identify and develop your Reader Panel. This is your team of hand-picked, knowledgeable, experts who will read and critique your essays. (More follows on this panel in the following section.)

The final reason is because some colleges read applications "real time." These colleges have something called "rolling admissions" which means they will render admissions decisions as they review applications.

For these reasons, don't wait until the last minute to write and edit your essays! I recommend students begin their essays as soon as the application goes "live" online. If you begin your essay on August 1, you can easily write a few drafts (with more than one version; see "Compose Two Distinct Versions" below), provide the drafts to your Reader Panel (see

"The Reader Panel" below), and finalize before returning to school for the fall semester.

> **Tip!**
> If you are feeling stuck, anxious, and have been procrastinating, go straight to Chapter 4, "*Los Huesos*: The Bones."

Seek Advice from Qualified Experts

The "expert" I am referring to is an individual who will coach you in designing and building your essay's theme, tone, and content. This individual should have a proven track record of successfully coaching students with content designed for selective college admissions. Don't get this confused with your Reader Panel (see next section). You need one expert to assist you with the conceptual framework (theme, content), and your Reader Panel to review your draft essay.

What if you don't have access to an expert? Many Latino students do not have the discretionary income to hire a professional consultant, nor do they attend highly-resourced high schools that offers this type of service. This is *precisely* why I wrote this book! Consider this book as your personal expert, to guide and assist you in developing ideal content.

Why it's Important to Obtain Help from an Expert

My students often write to me to share essay-writing advice and wisdom they've been offered. Some students have been told to try to sound sophisticated to impress the reader. Others have been told to convey an "All American" theme, downplaying their "Mexican-ness" and emphasizing their patriotism and love of country. Recently, I heard a whammy: A student should *never* disclose where they live in their essay. Hmm. As you can see, the advice you receive will reflect the expertise of the person you ask.

I hear so many stories like these from students each year, from well-meaning people. Be it teachers, relatives, or other folks, they all have an opinion regarding what they "feel" is a good essay. Keep in mind that many individuals (including English teachers) are not familiar with the complexity and competitiveness of the college admissions landscape.

Writing a "good" essay (proper grammar, well structured, etc.) and writing an exceptional essay that is *marketable for selective college admissions* are very different concepts. Unless the individual has qualified expertise in developing content and themes for selective college essays, it is risky to rely on his/her advice. When in doubt, ask the individual how they developed their opinion. Has s/he conducted significant research in this area, and can they support their claim with factual information such as success metrics? Do they serve on admissions teams for selective universities? Do they track student essays each year, and then compare them with the yield of admits, denied, and waitlisted at selective campuses? What is their evidence to support their assertion?

My point is that for something as critical as your college application essay, you should identify a *qualified* individual with expertise and knowledge in writing essays for *selective colleges*. A qualified College Admissions Consultant can advise the student based on knowledge, research, empirical evidence, and statistical proof. Our business depends on our knowledge and success — so we advise students based on what we know works (and help them avoid what doesn't work). A qualified College Admissions Consultant knows that there is not a single rule or "one size fits all" model for every student. Each student's profile is unique, and therefore, warrants a unique approach within their essay.

The Reader Panel:
Soliciting Feedback from the *Right* Group of Readers

After you've read the essay-writing strategies and methods in this book, and have drafted your essay theme and content, you will need a panel of readers to evaluate your draft essay.

If I am trying to get into the best university, I am going to seek the best readers to review, critique, and edit my essay. That makes sense, right? Yet, how many students give their essays to their friends, family members, and other people who are not experts at essay reading — or writing, for that matter! I guarantee if you ask your mom to critique your essay, she will say, "*Mija*, this is the best essay I've ever read! You are definitely going to get accepted to every college!"

Unless your friends and family members are AP or IB English teachers, college English professors, or college admissions coaches, don't recruit them for this important task. Instead, ask your AP or IB English teacher to review your essay. Also, consider giving your essay to a community college English instructor, a university English professor, a local business person, or your school counselor. When soliciting your reader panel, you will be asking these individuals to focus and comment on the following:

1. Is the tone in my essay appropriate for the prompt?
2. Does my essay have a nice rhythm? Does it flow?
3. Does it elicit a strong positive reaction? Does the reader feel inspired?
4. Does it sound like my authentic voice?
5. It is full of political hot buttons? Is it offensive?
6. Did I answer the question or prompt? Is my answer clearly identified?
7. Did I fully convey I have the *ganas* to get the job done?

Once you've identified your Reader Panel, you will need to establish due dates and set expectations. Provide your panel member with enough notice to respond to your request and to make arrangements to receive hard-copies of your essays. Two weeks is a reasonable amount of time for your panel member to review your essay and answer the seven questions you provided. Arrange for a day and time that you will pick-up your essays and discuss their feedback.

Finally, give a small token of appreciation to your panel member. Perhaps a hand-written card, with a $5 gift card? Sending a text or email message as a gesture of "thanks" is not a thoughtful way to express your gratitude.

Recap: The Reader Panel

Step 1: *After* receiving assistance from a qualified expert in the development of your draft essay theme and content, you will identify your panel of readers.

Step 2: Identify your Reader Panel by August 1.

Step 3: Provide ample notice to Panel.

Step 4: Establish a reasonable deadline.

Step 5: Provide Panel with critique/review questions.

Step 6: Show appreciation through a gift (thank them!).

Plagiarism

What is plagiarism? In a nutshell, plagiarism is (a) using another person's words or ideas without properly citing your source(s); and (b) taking another person's work and attempting to pass it off as your own. It doesn't matter whether you intentionally or unintentionally commit plagiarism. Colleges do not take plagiarism lightly. If you are caught plagiarizing you are at risk that your college application will be rejected.

High school students may not yet be familiar with the electronic plagiarism company Turnitin.com — phonetically, *turn it in* whose tagline is "The global leader in plagiarism prevention and online grading." This company, and several other "admission context verifiers" analyze the submissions of candidate applications for college admission, scholarships, and other programs. In fact, here is a statement directly from the fall 2015 Application Supplement at Harvard University:

Please be aware that Harvard, like most schools, uses outside companies to help process, review and collect data for applications. For this purpose we share application materials and information with them. Examples of such outside companies include the Common Application, transcript request services, and services that review materials for plagiarism. These companies in many cases will retain the application information in their databases. We also share application information with our alumni interviewers.

Apparently, many students "borrow" text from the internet for their essays. Don't resort to plagiarism for this important step in your academic career. Instead, follow this simple rule to be safe:

If you use a quote, properly cite the quote. Here is an example: As the late César Chavez said, *"The end of all education should surely be service to others."* In this example, you are citing the name of the person who is credited with the original statement and using quotation marks to denote your use of quoted material. Your essay should reflect your unique voice. Avoid borrowing thoughts, concepts, or words from others.

A well-written essay is tempting for others to pilfer. Therefore, it is not advisable to text portions, or send your essay electronically (if you can avoid it). Do not post on Facebook! If a college admissions department receives *two identical essays*, it will be obvious that one of the two (or both) were plagiarized. The admissions team cannot determine which of the two candidates plagiarized, so both candidates may be disqualified.

From Draft to "Submit"

Students will hate the sentence I'm about to write. Here it goes: *It will take you several rounds of drafts before you have a polished essay worthy of submission to universities.*

Students believe they can sit down, crank out a draft essay, send it to their mom, make a few edits, spell check, and submit! I wish it were that easy — but it's not.

For the students I coach, on average we go through *at least* five rounds of edits before we get to the point of taking it to the Reader Panel. Five rounds? Yep. That means we construct our first draft for content and theme. In our second draft we put together our beginning, middle, and end of the story. The third draft is where we add the technical details. In the fourth draft we tackle the rhetorical devices to add flair to the essay. And, in the fifth draft — and sometimes the most important phase — we look at the rhythm and flow. We read through it, out loud, and tweak words here and there. We also determine whether we need to eliminate words to meet our word limit.

That seems like a lot of work, right? But, it's worth it. My students who go through this rigorous process are winning national scholarships and gaining admission to the best universities. Skipping these steps will leave you with an unpolished essay, unworthy of submission to selective universities.

Compose Two Distinct Essays

Although certainly not required, you may wish to create at least two distinct (*different*) Personal Statements. This means having two essay renditions responding to the same prompt, or two essay renditions responding to two different prompts. Why? In my experience, students who compose more than one essay will often come up with a more compelling essay that stands out and will be suitable for admission purposes. Upon review by your Reader Panel, one essay will likely shine.

I encourage my students to show their essay renditions to others outside of their Reader Panel to see if there is consensus. If eight out of ten readers chose the same essay, then you can feel confident you are submitting the superior essay. In addition, there are perks for students writing and comparing more than one essay. This often results in a "combo" strategy, where a combination of parts from essay one and parts from essay two can be joined together for a more powerful and appealing essay. And, the additional essay may be suitable for a future scholarship essay.

Avoid Regurgitating the Application

What do I mean by "regurgitating" your application? A regurgitated application will sound like this in an essay:

> *In my freshman year I completed pre-AP English and Honors Math. Then, in my sophomore year I took three AP courses and one Conceptual Physics course at my local community college. In addition, I also completed 340 hours of community service for the following organizations . . .*

Your test scores, academic curricula, and extracurricular activities will already be listed on your completed College Application. There is no need to repeat these details in your essay. The point of your essay is to introduce yourself, in a personal way, to the admissions reader. Focus instead on sharing interesting details you have not already disclosed in your application.

The exception is when you have developed a strong thesis and wish to include a few details to support your thesis. This is perfectly fine. For example, if your essay illustrates an analogy of your "before" and "after" academic profile, then adding academic details to compare and contrast would be highly effective.

Or, if your essay talks about how you had an epiphany in your sophomore year and turned your grades around, then you should include details of your GPA and/or coursework completed.

Or, if your essay theme revolves around your altruism (volunteering/community service), then it would make sense to add quantifiable details concerning the names of organizations, description of your service, and the number of hours you served in that capacity.

Recap
Start your essay in early August.
Use a qualified expert to construct theme and content.
Develop your Reader Panel.
Avoid plagiarism.
Take time to go through the revision process.
Consider composing at least two distinct essays.
Avoid regurgitating the application.

Now that we have covered the logistics of the college essay, let's consider how we will select the right prompt.

Selecting the Right Prompt

For a small group of colleges, including the University of California system, you will not have the flexibility to select a prompt that suits you. What? Yep, they pre-designate the prompts you must answer. Below are the pre-designated 2014/2015 prompts for the University of California. You have 1,000 words total to respond to both prompts:

The University of California 2014 Prompt No. 1
Describe the world you come from — for example, your family, community or school — and tell us how your world has shaped your dreams and aspirations.

The University of California 2014 Prompt No. 2
Tell us about a personal quality, talent, accomplishment, contribution or experience that is important to you. What about this quality or accomplishment makes you proud and how does it relate to the person you are?

That's the University of California. What if you are applying to a college on the Common Application? Great news! You get to pick the prompt! Fortunately, they give you the option to select from one of five prompts. But, how do you know which one to pick?

Let's look at the Common Application prompts for the 2014/2015 application cycle. You will select only one prompt, and your statement will be sent to all of the colleges you select that use the Common Application. I will share my feedback following each prompt including "pros" and "cons" and the "bottom line."

Common Application Prompt No. 1
Some students have a background or story that is so central to their identity that they believe their application would be incomplete without it. If this sounds like you, then please share your story.

Pros: The pro I see here is that the majority of students reading this book will have incredible stories worth telling. In this prompt, you have full reign to capture your unique background. This prompt is also a perfect segue to exemplify your cultural authenticity. Because many

Latino students embrace their ethnic heritage, this is central to their identity and worth discussing.

Cons: The con I see is that it conveys a sense of urgency. The reader is, understandably, expecting the essay to be extraordinarily compelling. If the student is unable to convey something "so central to their identity" and misses the mark, his/her essay will be lackluster.

Bottom line? Consider this prompt if you truly have a compelling background or story *and* can confidently articulate the significance of your unique background or story to enhance or complement your profile. Remember to include culturally authentic details!

Common Application Prompt No. 2

Recount an incident or time when you experienced failure. How did it affect you, and what lessons did you learn?

Pros: This is a fairly straightforward prompt. The pro here is that many of us have experienced failure at some point, so it is quite easy to recollect such an experience. The other pro is that citing a failure gives us the opportunity to demonstrate how we overcame the obstacle, thus turning a negative into a positive. Taking a failure and turning it around demonstrates maturity, creativity, and a clear and purposeful vision.

Cons: The con I see is that some high school students may be naively honest. Some students may recall topics or themes that are not advisable within a Personal Statement (see Chapter 11, *Top Ten Mistakes Students Make*). Or, some students may be too candid in discussing his/her response to a particular failure, and may unintentionally convey negative personal qualities. Some of these negative qualities may include immaturity, selfishness, and simple-mindedness, to name a few. Let me give you an example.

Let's say Hector wrote about his low performance on an SAT examination. Hector might say that he was disappointed in himself because he felt his score was a "failure." Hector might go on to say he believed his score would lower his chances of admission to a prestigious university. While his logic may be true, it could convey that Hector values social status over learning, not something a student should highlight in a college essay.

Instead, Hector may want to elaborate and discuss how he engaged in reflective analysis. In doing so, Hector arrived at another conclusion. His conclusion was that the short-term result was an inferior examination score. However, his long-term conclusion was a valuable lesson about preparing for such exams. He could concede that although he is bright, he should have participated in a preparation program, joined a study group, or practiced on-line drills. This type of conclusion would demonstrate Hector's maturity, strategic and critical thinking skills, and his ability to see the "bigger picture."

Bottom line? The focus should be on *how* the student responded to the failure, not the failure itself. Universities are interested in knowing how a student perceives her/himself, responds to life's unfortunate events, and successfully navigates challenging situations. In other words, they want to know whether a student will manage duress, and the degree to which they have developed skills and a resilient mindset to overcome potential obstacles. Students who are reflective thinkers and writers may wish to consider this prompt. To view an example for this prompt, see Daniel Morataya's essay, "From Tragedy to Triumph" in Part Six.

Common Application Prompt No. 3: *Reflect on a time when you challenged a belief or idea. What prompted you to act? Would you make the same decision again?*

Pros: For most students I believe this prompt will be the most challenging, yet the most appealing. It presents a challenge because "belief" systems are hot buttons for many of us. I like this prompt because it requires the student to quantify and qualify the situation, rather than speculating or theorizing.

Cons: Not knowing the politics of your reader, it may be risky for a student to candidly expose his/her beliefs or philosophical ideals. On the other hand — this is *precisely* what universities encourage. They hope to attract students who challenge the status quo, go against the grain, question societal norms, take action, and ultimately change our world.

Bottom line? The beauty of this question is that it hinges on how the student *acted*. It separates an ideal from an action; thinking versus doing. Students who can demonstrate they have *ganas* or conviction and have taken a stand may want to consider this prompt. To view a wonderful response to this prompt, read Amber Escobar's essay, "Political Asylum as a Transgender Teen" in Part Six.

Common Application Prompt No. 4

Describe a place or environment where you are perfectly content. What do you do or experience there, and why is it meaningful to you?

Pros: One way to approach this prompt is to consider that the place or environment need not be limited to a physical place. It could be a figurative "place" representing the student's "passion." For example, it could be a passion for solving mathematical formulas, painting murals, playing varsity soccer, or teaching English Language Learners. The student may feel perfectly content within these environments because that is where his/her passion lies. Or, it could be the place where the student escapes (mentally) — where the environment is the imagination. You can see that this prompt is limitless — allowing students to creatively describe their unique interests and passion.

Cons: There is a fine line in semantics here. Being "perfectly content" could convey passion or complacency, depending on the essay. In other words, if you are "perfectly content" does that mean you are not consistently striving toward excellence? World leaders never settle for "content" — they continually seek excellence. Carefully select your words.

Bottom line? The critical phrase here is, "why is it *meaningful* to you?" In responding to this prompt, it is not enough to describe the place or environment. You must tell the reader what you experience in that "space" and why and how it has impacted you in a meaningful way.

Common Application Prompt No. 5

Discuss an accomplishment or event, formal or informal, that marked your transition from childhood to adulthood within your culture, community, or family.

Pros: This is an opportunity to demonstrate maturity or to discuss an intellectual growth spurt. This is also an opportunity to expand upon an activity listed within your application — such as an internship, leadership program, or community service activity.

Cons: It is narrowly focused. The parameters of time and place within this narrow context create unnecessary limitations for the writer. Unfortunately, I foresee hackneyed essays such as "My Bat Mitzvah" or "*Mi Quinceañera.*" However, you will see clever responses to this prompt by superstars Rafael Garibay (UCLA) and Michelle Benavidez (Yale) in Part Six.

If you're still stuck and can't figure out which prompt is best for you, here are my bottom line recommendations:

1. Represent you in the best light — one that allows you to speak to your best qualities, strengths, and assets;
2. Align the prompt with your personal story — one that easily flows with the narrative you'd prefer to write about; and
3. Make the writing process as easy as possible — one that feels right and inspires you.

Most of all, pick the prompt that will share something wonderful about you that has not already been shared within your application!

Recycling or "Re-Purposing" Essays?

"Can't I just use an essay I've already written, change a few words, and re-purpose for other prompts?"

Well, yeah. Certainly, you can cut and paste a few paragraphs. However, I don't advise it. Here's why:

Re-purposing an essay is like borrowing your sister's prom dress. Just because it fits, doesn't mean you should wear it. You have your own distinctive style and her dress may not suit you. Ditto with a previously written essay: the essay was written to respond to a very specific question – not to cut and paste and force into a new response. Furthermore, it may take more time in the long run to re-arrange text and paragraphs, rather than starting from scratch. You get one shot to tell your story. Do you want your story to be a cut-and-paste mock up job? Or, do you want to "nail it"?

Now that we've looked at the University of California prompts and the Common Application prompts, here are prompts representing colleges that use their own proprietary application (and essays):

Georgetown 2014 Prompt

"As Georgetown is a diverse community, the Admissions Committee would like to know more about you in your own words. Please submit a brief essay, either personal or creative, which you feel best describes you."

MIT Fall 2014 Prompt

"What attribute of your personality are you most proud of, and how has it impacted your life so far? This could be your creativity, effective leadership, sense of humor, integrity, or anything else you'd like to tell us about."

Rutgers 2014 Prompt

"Rutgers University is a vibrant community of people with a wide variety of backgrounds and experiences. How would you benefit from and contribute to such an environment? Consider variables such as your talents, travels, leadership activities, volunteer services, and cultural experiences."

As you can see, the University of California, the Common Application, and the non-participating colleges have different prompts. However, regardless of the prompt, they are all asking the same thing: Why and how are you unique? Tell them!

Recap
Review each prompt carefully.
Select the prompt that complements your profile.
Consider "pros" and "cons" of Common Application prompts.
Avoid "re-purposing" (recycling) an essay!

Regardless of the prompt selected, to develop an exceptional essay follow the guidelines and strategies in this book. To see actual essays responding to the Common Application and University of California prompts, see Part Six, *"Putting it All Together — Sample Essays."*

Part Two

The Mechanics of
the Personal Statement

4

Los Huesos - The Bones

*I*f you are short on time, panicking, riddled with anxiety, and struggling to get started, forget the rest of this book and focus on this chapter: *Los Huesos*.

The Bones are simply that — the most basic and fundamental structural components of your essay. This concept forces you to sort through the gibberish and get to your main point. Students mistakenly believe they must approach their college essay with critical analysis and eloquent sophistication. However, the key to beginning your essay is just the opposite. It's to simplify. In fact, read what these folks says about the genius of simplicity:

"If you can't explain it simply, you don't understand it well enough."
— Albert Einstein

"Life is really simple, but we insist on making it complicated."
— Confucius

"Simplicity is the ultimate sophistication."
— Leonardo da Vinci

Now, grab a pen and some college-lined paper, *y siéntate.* Let's consider this prompt from the Fall 2014/2015 Common Application:

> *Some students have a background or story that is so central to their identity that they believe their application would be incomplete without it. If this sounds like you, then please share your story.*

Identify the Question(s) — The first thing you will do is identify how many questions the prompt contains. I see two questions, plus an *indirect* question. An *indirect* question? *¡No te preocupes!* — the definition of an *indirect* question follows shortly.

Question 1
"What *is* the background or story that is central to my identity?

Question 2
How did this background/story influence me?

Indirect Question
What does this have to do with my candidacy as a college applicant?
In other words, how does this relate to my aspiration to attend college?

The Indirect Question — Before we proceed, let's look at the definition of an indirect question. An indirect question is the unstated, implied question within a prompt. Identifying the indirect question requires the student to ask, "What is this prompt *really* asking of me?" It forces the student to consider the "bigger picture" or angle derived from the prompt.

Let's get back to our example. Without over thinking, just answer the questions from the prompt. No intro, no fancy thesis. Be clear and concise. Here is an example:

1. My background is that I come from eight generations of *hierberas* (herbalists).

2. My background shapes the way I view modern medicine, indigenous culture, and ecological sustainability.

3. My background influenced my decision to pursue plant biology as an undergraduate.

Here is another 2014/2015 Common Application prompt as an example:

Recount an incident or time when you experienced failure. How did it affect you, and what lessons did you learn?

What's the first thing we do here? We identify the number of questions in the prompt. I see three, plus an *indirect* question:

Question 1
"Recount an incident"

Question 2
How did it affect me?

Question 3
What lessons did I learn?

Indirect Question
What does this have to do with my candidacy for college?

Let's break this down, following *Los Huesos* strategy:

1. In spring 2014 I experienced failure. A heckler interrupted my speech for Class President.

2. The heckler threw off my balance; I felt angry and defensive.

3. I learned three* lessons from this experience: Stay calm and composed, sense of humor is a must, and the response to adversity matters most. *See Chapter 5, *The Magical Power of Three.*

4. This lesson taught me how to remain disciplined in challenging situations, such as in the challenge of transitioning to a competitive university.

To see this essay fleshed out, go to Chapter 6, "The Personal Statement is Like a *Taco de Carne Asada.*"

It can't be that simple, right? Yes. It *is* that simple. The problem is we spend way too much time worrying about whether our essay will appear clever, insightful, and intellectual; and we miss the big picture. We first have to answer the question by gathering our bones. Trust me, and use this strategy *before* you begin writing.

Once you have your bones, use the strategies in *The Personal Statement is Like a Taco de Carne Asada* to expand and add "flesh" to your essay.

Recap
Read the prompt and identify the number of questions asked.
Pay attention to the indirect question asked.
Answer the questions succinctly.
Don't overanalyze!
Your answers will become the "bones" of your essay.

5

The Magical Power of Three

When I first began coaching students in writing expository essays, I knew the power of three was a great practical model. The neatly structured "three supporting paragraphs" fit perfectly within this context. It wasn't until later that I noticed the significant impact of the "three" strategy in college admission essays. It seems that across cultures, geography, and time, we humans seem to have this strong preference for things in three.

For example, consider competitions: First, Second, and Third places. Or, what about corporate entities like ABC, CBS, AT&T, or 3M? Even our 24-hour day is broken up into three parts: morning, noon, and night. Again, the magic three. Even our life cycles are segmented into threes: infancy, adolescence, and adulthood. What about, "Third time's a charm." Three Wise Men, Three Stooges, Three Musketeers, Three Amigos? Perhaps one is too little, and more than three is too much?

"Three" is magical in essay writing because it sounds definitive, conveys careful and thoughtful analysis, and does not overwhelm the reader. See, I did it just there. I just gave you three reasons, and it sounded convincing! To respond effectively to a "Tell us why" essay, let's consider the power of three. What does this look like in an essay? Here are some examples:

"My reasons are three-fold . . ."
"There are three critical reasons I chose to . . ."
"I've learned three things from this experience . . ."

When implementing a "three" reasons strategy, try to consider three critical angles. For students, this means to respond by considering academic, personal, and other influences. If you understand the power of three, you can use it effectively in your essay writing.

For example, if we consider a few of the 2014/2015 Common Application prompts, we can see how the Magical Power of Three works perfectly within this context:

Prompt: *Recount an incident or time when you experienced failure. How did it affect you, and what lessons did you learn?*

Magical Power of Three: Tell them three (3) lessons you learned from this experience. For example, perhaps you developed a new skill, or gained a new perspective, or the experience was a catalyst for some other endeavor.

Prompt: *Describe a place or environment where you are perfectly content. What do you do or experience there, and why is it meaningful to you?*

Magical Power of Three: Tell them three (3) reasons why the environment and experience is meaningful to you. For example, perhaps the environment stimulates your creativity, or that it is a calm or serene escape from a stressful life circumstance, or that it helps you to remain focused on your academic or personal goals.

Recap

The Magical Power of Three sounds definitive, conveys careful and thoughtful analysis, and does not overwhelm the reader.

Human beings seems to have a preference for things in threes!

This structure lends itself to many college essay prompts.

6

The Personal Statement is Like a Taco de Carne Asada

N ow that you've got *Los Huesos*, you are ready to add flesh to your essay. This chapter explains how crafting a Personal Statement is similar to preparing a *Taco de Carne Asada*.

Déjame explicarte. You wouldn't fry up tortillas only to discover you have no *carne*. And, everyone knows a taco is not a taco without the extra "stuff" that makes it *delicioso*. I'm talking about *el sabór* — the flavor or kick from the *cebolla, cilantro, limón, y chilé*.

Think of your essay as a taco. To understand the power of the taco, we need to approach each component separately. Let's begin with the shell.

The Corn Tortilla or "Taco Shell"

The corn tortilla is the "shell" of the essay—containing the introductory paragraph and the closing thoughts. We'll get to the closing thoughts in a moment. First, let's talk about how to introduce your topic. The corn tortilla compels the reader to pick it up and take a bite! Therefore, your corn tortilla (or introductory paragraph) should be as compelling as possible. This is where you will beckon the Admissions reader to take notice.

If you follow my strategy, "TIN CASA" you know a compelling introduction is achieved by one of three methods: Use a quote, tell a story, or answer a question. See Chapter 7 "TIN CASA" for detailed information and examples of compelling introductions. What would this look like in a Common Application prompt? Let's refer to the Common Application prompt we responded to in *Los Huesos* — The Bones (Chapter 4):

Prompt No. 2
Recount an incident or time when you experienced failure.
How did it affect you, and what lessons did you learn?

1. A heckler interrupted my Class President speech.
2. The heckler threw off my balance; I felt angry and defensive.
3. I learned 3 lessons.

Joaquin is going to use the Storytelling strategy to create a compelling taco shell:

On this warm spring morning, the auditorium was packed with fidgety and talkative high school students. This annual ritual of what Principal Mendoza calls, "Oratory Excellence" is the forum where students elect a Class President. When Principal Mendoza announced my name, the room quieted as I walked to the podium. I was the only Latino candidate — in the history of our mostly white campus to run for President. In auto pilot mode, I checked my watch, adjusted my tie, and took a deep breath. I was ready.

Although each candidate was only allowed two minutes to articulate key points, I was fully prepared. I had enlisted the help from our Speech & Debate team — learning signature moves like the "rhetorical negative assertion" and the "rhythmic verbal dance." I spent weeks listening to tape recordings of my speech to perfect my tone, rhythm, and punctuate key points. I watched video tapes of my speech, without audio, so that I could identify distracting movements or overly animated hand gestures. Sí, estaba listo.

However, through all of my preparation and rehearsing, I failed to account for one obstacle: a heckler. Apparently, a student in the audience felt compelled to interrupt my speech by yelling, "Go back to Mexico!" I was devastated. This person threw me for a moment as I did not know how to respond. In what seemed like several minutes (although it was actually only seconds), I quickly surveyed my options. I could retort with a clever insult, ignore the interruption, or ask administration to remove the hostile student.

That was an introduction. It sets the stage, captures attention, and gives just enough details to hook the reader. This taco shell is enticing, and the reader wants to know more about this speech. In the section below we will see how Joaquin built the rest of his taco.

Now, what about the rest of us? Yeah, those of us who have never stood in front of a 3,000 student body or scored a winning touchdown? Most students will not have a story like this, so it is important to understand that our everyday life experiences can also come alive through the use of descriptive details.

So, let's look at a more identifiable story. In the next paragraph, see how Graciela uses the "Storytelling" technique as her "*shell*" for a compelling introduction:

When I was seven, my family emigrated to the U.S. from the small village of El Remolino, in the municipality of Juchipila, Zacatecas, Mexico. We settled in Firebaugh, California — a small, rural, agricultural town surrounded by mountains and fields. Shortly after our arrival, my parents enrolled me in first grade. I was placed in an English Learner Development (ELD) program called "Structured English Immersion." I can still recall verbalizing words like "cup" and "cat" as I struggled to correctly pronounce these seemingly simple words. However, my true struggle was during my proficiency assessments. I desperately wanted to advance from ELD to a mainstream classroom, so I placed a lot of pressure on myself to obtain a qualifying score. I would become excessively nervous during these assessment tests — grinding my teeth on No. 2 pencils and breaking off the erasers. Through all the gnawing and chewing, I failed many assessment exams and did not advance to mainstream English until the 6th grade.

Graciela took a fairly common experience for many English Language students, and used storytelling to bring the reader into her world. We understand her frustration, and eagerly anticipate the subsequent paragraphs where she recounts how she eventually advanced to AP English.

The *Carne* or "Meat" of the Taco

The *carne asada* is the meat of our essay, providing the proof or examples of what we claimed in the introductory paragraph. For example, in our student body speech, we expect Joaquin to provide back-up details in the subsequent paragraphs. However, if Joaquin does not elaborate or provide details, then his tortilla has no *carne*! Read the following Fall 2014/2015 Common Application prompt:

Recount an incident or time when you experienced failure. How did it affect you, and what lessons did you learn?

How would you respond? To start, let's tell the reader *how* it affected us. In the *Los Huesos* exercise, we said: *The heckler threw off my balance; I felt angry and defensive.*

So, let's add the *carne* by expressing our emotions. We want to list the emotions in the natural order in which they would have occurred. Why are we talking about emotions here? Because we need the emotional pull — to get the reader fully engaged. We do this to convey our experience in a visceral way.

When I heard those four words, "Go back to Mexico" I felt as though I were dreaming. I heard the words, but they seemed fuzzy and distant. My anger quickly snapped me back to reality. I was angry and defensive, and wasn't sure how I would manage this ordeal. The microphone was clipped to the left side of my sports coat lapel — near my heart. Could they hear my rapidly thumping heartbeat? While my heart was thumping, there was a battle going between my gut and brain. My gut nudged me to call out the jerk publicly and humiliate him. I wanted to self-righteously proclaim, "I'm not even Mexican — I'm Salvadorean." I was a skilled orator, after all — El Rey de "Retort." I could do this as easily as I could recite Neruda's Song of Despair. However, I fought my urge to satisfy my ego, gained composure, and devised an alternate response.

In this paragraph, Joaquin provided *carne* to illustrate effectively *how* the incident affected him. He didn't simply say, "It affected me." Instead, he provided visceral details to give us a glimpse into his state of mind. In his closing paragraphs he will discuss the three lessons he learned. See Joaquin's conclusion at the end of this chapter: The Conclusion — the Finishing Touch of our *Taco*.

For our ELD student Graciela, let's consider how she provided the *carne* to back up her introductory paragraph:

After failing to advance from ESL to mainstream English classes, I began to feel defeated. I wanted to assimilate as quickly as possible, so that I would be viewed by my classmates as a competent English speaker. Because I wasn't progressing as quickly as I wished, I started to doubt my intellectual abilities. I began to resent my daily walk into Classroom 210, and the sound of Ms. Ayala's daily greeting: iBuenos Dias, Estudiantes! It had already been four years, and my confidence was whittling away. Each fall, my heart would sink when I viewed the class rosters posted on the glass window of our administration office.

Graciela added *carne* to her essay by backing up her introductory paragraph with evidence.

Another clever way to add *carne* to your taco is to quantify or qualify your introductory statement or thesis. You do this by providing technical details. For example, let's say Julian formed a *Latinos Unidos* club at his high school in Fresno, California. In his introduction, he might talk about the reasons *why* he formed the club and *how* he was able to organize it. But, so what? We need Julian to tell us the impact of his organization. To do this, Julian needs to share technical details that quantify the club's impact:

> *That first year, my team and I organized three major events. We facilitated two fundraising campaigns, and one school-wide celebration. Our first campaign helped raise funds for our local Migrant Ministries. Through a tamale sale and pan dulce bake-off, we raised $8,000 . . .*

The Flavor of the *Taco*
¡El Sabór!

Any *taco* worth its *frijoles* must have flavor or ¡*sabór*! The flavor comes from the "fixins" —the *cebolla, cilantro, limón, y chile*. The flavor of your essay comes from special additions or "flair" used for effect. The flavor of your essay may be achieved through the use of rhetorical devices, narrative style, tone, or a combination of several literary tools. These are just fancy words to say that the way you structure your words and convey language in your essay will impact your reader.

In this section I will demonstrate a few techniques to spice up your essay. We will review descriptive language, honing the senses, and the use of analogy.

Descriptive Language — Descriptive language paints a picture for your reader. It describes a situation or experience, with details and technical terms. Adjectives are your friends in descriptive language — helping you bring life to your words.

For example, instead of saying "The cake was good," you can add descriptive language to help your reader envision the cake: *"In every bite of Tres Leches cake I savored the densely spongy cake, heavenly fresh cream, and dusting of aromatic cinnamon."* When we read the descriptive language in the second sentence, we can almost taste the cake, right? This is what we aim for in our college essay: we want the reader to join us. Invite the reader into your story by providing descriptive language.

Another way to add descriptive language is to provide technical terms. In this way, we can qualify our topic. For example, if we are talking about a "final tennis match" our job is to convey the significance of the tournament. Instead of "final tennis match," we might say: "The Northern California Interscholastic Federation (CIF) State Tennis Championship." By adding those technical details, we escalate the prestige of the tournament and thereby the significance of the experience. You might also add that audience members were head coaches of "NCAA Division I Tennis teams" to enhance the drama. A tiny detail goes a long way! We will learn more about the use of Descriptive Language within Chapter 7, TIN CASA ("A" for "Audience").

Honing the Senses — Honing the senses is an effective way to engage the reader by providing vivid, sensory details. This allows the reader to more closely interpret and imagine the writer's perspective and experience. To "hone the senses" just imagine the five senses we were taught in grade school: sight, smell, sound, taste, and touch. When describing the context of your situation, refer to at least a few of these senses within your essay. For example:

> *As we drive into Tijuana, I immediately recognize the smell of fried lengua and cesos. My eyes scan the perpetual grey skies, Taqueros on every street corner, and Tejuino vendors peddling their elixirs. Dogs and children run through the streets, ignoring the stench of raw sewage.*

In this example, Vanessa honed the senses by using the sense of smell and sight to describe her drive through *Tijuana*.

Use of Analogy — An analogy is a literary device that compares and contrasts two dissimilar things by establishing a relationship based on similarities. It is a highly effective persuasive-writing technique used in Personal Statements. The key to nailing this technique is to construct your argument in a parallel manner.

Let's review how Raquel added *sabór* through the use of an analogy. In this final, closing paragraph, Raquel compares her aspiration to become a genetics researcher with the practicality and necessity of working at McDonalds:

> *While recombinant strands of DNA and using gel electrophoresis is worlds away from wrapping burgers and asking whether it will be a dollar menu*

item or happy meal, these two unique worlds describe where I come from and where I wish to be. I have dreams that extend beyond the Golden Arches. As a high school student my work and home life fed my body, but now I will pursue undergraduate studies in genetics to feed my soul. Ten years from now my hope is to be filling a gel for genetics research instead of filling the vat for French Fries.

The Conclusion – the Finishing Touch of our *Taco*

So, we've got our introduction, the *carne*, and we've added the fixins – *el sabór*. But, what about the other side of our *taco*? After all, we're not talking about a one-sided, flat *tostada*. A *taco* has two sides, right? In our taco analogy we've only covered one side of our *taco*, the introduction. Now, we'll look at the other side of our *taco*, the conclusion.

The conclusion paragraph in a college application essay is *not* like the conclusions most students are used to writing in high school. For example, you would never say: "In conclusion, . . ." in your college essay.

So, how do we approach the last paragraph? If you've reviewed the sample essays at the end of this book you can see that successful students do three things:

1. Succinctly restate main points by recalling the *carne* or "proof" referenced in the preceding paragraphs;
2. Answer the indirect question, "What does this have to do with my candidacy (qualifications) as an aspiring college applicant?; and

3. End with a positive twist — the final statement should leave the reader feeling optimistic and inspired.

Earlier in this chapter we read about Joaquin, the candidate for Class President. He was heckled during his speech and shared how the incident affected him. Considering the three angles above, let's see how Joaquin "nailed" his essay in the conclusion:

Although being heckled during my Class President speech was not a positive experience, I did learn three very important things. First, I learned that having a sense of humor is important. I have come to realize that humor and lack of sensitivity are not mutually exclusive. While I can appreciate the complexities of racism and human behavior, I don't have to internalize racist incidents and react negatively to every episode. I can address complex issues in a thoughtful and sensitive manner, but I can also have a sense of humor to help me maintain a positive perspective.

Second, I learned that taking things personally can be destructive. Looking back at the heckler incident, I came to realize his outburst was not necessarily about me or my speech. The outburst represented his anger, immaturity, lack of respect, and lack of knowledge.

Finally, I learned that the way we respond to a situation can determine our future success. By maintaining a rational and balanced perspective and finding humor in challenging moments, I am better prepared for unforeseen circumstances at my future college campus.

Now, let's look at three examples of strong conclusions from additional student essays:

Conclusion Example 1:

Like Canelo, I have been the underdog with a fighting spirit. I have looked at my opponent, square in the eyes, and did not shy away. Rather than succumbing to defeat, or conceding life, my many obstacles have positively influenced my goals, decisions, and actions. The culmination of how I have responded to these circumstances has made me a stronger person. As I look ahead to my life as an undergraduate student, I am prepared to tackle any unforeseen challenges and succeed. My resilience, strength, and commitment to my educational goals will render me undefeated. Moving forward, I am no longer an unprepared fighter. I am a skilled pugilist, equipped with the tools, strategies, and spirit to triumph. As the great Muhammad Ali once said, "If my mind can conceive it, and my heart can believe it − then I can achieve it."

Conclusion Example 2:

I am determined to achieve both of my undergraduate goals: to learn the theory of biological sciences and to explore the interrelation with our social environment. As an aspiring physician, I seek both perspectives to influence my future practice. For these reasons, I believe I would thrive as a student, scholar, scientist, and ecologist, in the College of Human Ecology.

Conclusion Example 3:

The combined influences and experiences − from my parent's wisdom, to my unique community environment, helped me to successfully transition from a high school student to a university researcher. During my summer internship I grew in many ways. I learned how it felt to be part of a team, to work amongst scholars, and to perform to the best of my abilities. However, the most important factor that influenced my transition this summer was realizing who I am and where I am going. As the daughter of immigrant, middle school educated, hard working parents, I will soon begin my undergraduate studies at a four-year university. I am looking forward to transitioning into the world of an undergraduate student — where I will again be wide-eyed, nervous, but eager.

Recap

From these sample conclusion paragraphs, you can see how each of these writers followed the same strategy:

Summed-up and re-stated their thesis.
Reinforced key points.
Related the experiences to their qualifications as a college applicant/candidate.
Ended with a powerful, positive twist.

To see many sample essays and review conclusion paragraphs, see "Putting it All Together — Sample Essays" in the final section of this book.

7

TIN CASA

M nemonic devices help students remember information and streamline the writing process. TIN CASA is a mnemonic tool I developed to help my students "check" themselves. This rubric is intended for use at *the end* of the writing process. This rubric is a useful tool for writing many types of essays including college applications, scholarships, internships, or leadership programs. Here is the acronym:

T = Tone
I = Intellectual
N = Narrative

C = Compelling Introduction
A = Answer the Prompt!
S = Speak to Your Audience
A = Authenticity (Cultural)

Tone. Tone is a weird thing. We can't touch it, but we can feel it. We certainly won't define it for our reader, but they will immediately recognize it. Tone is to an essay what oxygen is to humans: Your essay cannot survive without it.

Tone is critical because it does three things. First, it determines how your theme will be conveyed to the reader. Second, tone is a signifier.

It tells the reader the direction of your essay. Finally, tone does the one thing above all else that will make or break your essay. I think the late Maya Angelou best brings this point home:

> *"At the end of the day, people won't remember*
> *what you said or did. They will remember*
> *how you made them feel."*
> —Maya Angelou

That's all we need to know about tone: *It makes us feel.* Our goal is to make our reader feel great. By great, I mean positive, inspired, and optimistic. How do we set our tone? We do this through a few easy (but clever) ways.

First, we use carefully selected words to set the tone. For example, look at these two paragraphs:

> *Maria bit her lip, glanced at the clock, and began bouncing her foot under the library table.*

> *Jesus' father slammed the book on the table and said, "¿Quién hizo esto?"*

In both of these sentences, we can *feel* the character's emotion. Maria "*bit*" her lip and "*bounced*" her foot to convey nervous tension. Jesus' father "*slammed*" the book to convey anger.

Another way to convey tone is through a formal or informal writing style. How will the writing style affect your essay's tone? Let's find out.

Formal or Informal?

Should your tone be formal or informal? Generally, your tone should be somewhere in the middle. It shouldn't be so formal that it creates distance between you and your reader. Formality tends to be off-putting to readers because it conveys a "stiff" attitude and rigidness. More importantly, a rigid and formal tone may not represent your authentic voice. On the other hand, an informal tone may be too casual — conveying a lack of seriousness or respect.

Experienced and crafty writers may wish to use a less formal style for effect. For example, if they intend to narrate their essay in the form of a story, then it makes sense to use informal conventions like contractions and colloquial terms.

Humor or Sarcasm?

Conveying a sense of humor can be a useful strategy to convey a "light" tone and produce a strong, informal essay. However, inexperienced writers are often unskilled at using humor and sarcasm appropriately within their essays. It is a skill that takes a lot of practice and sophistication.

However, there are "safe" ways to infuse humor without the risk of offending your reader. One way is to introduce a humorous topic within your introductory paragraph. If you have a funny anecdotal reference, quote, or story, it may be an effective way to open your essay. However, limit the humor to your introductory paragraph — sticking to a less informal (non-humorous) tone for the remainder of your essay.

Sarcasm, as a strategy for producing tone, is even trickier. Using sarcasm may unintentionally convey *offensive* personal characteristics such as arrogance, contemptuousness, smugness, and — here's a great word — pomposity! Let's not go down that road.

Bottom line: The tone should be consistent with the prompt. In other words, you wouldn't use a silly and casual tone to respond to a serious question.

You don't need to establish your tone before you begin writing your essay. In fact, many times a particular tone will emerge once you start writing. For now, just know that the appropriate tone is somewhere between formal and informal (leaning toward informal). The tone you use will be determined by your writing style and abilities, and the topic of your essay.

The tone should also convey humility. It is perfectly fine for students to speak about their accomplishments as long as they maintain a humble tone. See Chapter 12 "Essays Gone Wrong!" for examples of essays that fail the humility test.

Tips to Convey Appropriate Tone
For a college essay, tone should be in the middle:
not too formal, but not too casual.
Experienced, gifted writers can be less formal.

Keep it light, friendly, and authentic.
Make it inspirational, uplifting, and optimistic.

Avoid

Avoid colloquialisms, sarcasm, or cheesy humor.

Avoid an inappropriately casual response to a serious prompt.

Avoid language that leads the reader to feel defensive, sad, or pity.

Intellectual. When writing their college essays, students often forget to use what I call, their "scholarly voice." The Personal Statement is *the* place where Latino students should demonstrate their intellectual curiosity and prowess. After all, they are scholars!

In using their "scholarly voice" students should try to connect their essay theme to their academic major; choose language that plays up and doesn't "dumb down" their essay; showcase their academic talents; and convey intelligence, but not conceit. Sounds simple, huh? It's actually somewhat tricky for students to showcase their awesome academic abilities without coming across as arrogant. To see an example of an overly confident and arrogant essay, see Chapter 12, "Essays Gone Wrong!"

Using your intellectual or scholarly voice can be accomplished in many ways. It can be conveyed through a complex topic or subject matter in your essay. For example, you might discuss the similarities between the riots and protests during the 1960's Civil Rights movement and the protests happening in 2014 at refugee detention facilities housing immigrant children. Or, you might discuss a fascinating lab experiment in your AP Biology or AP Chemistry course.

Interestingly, Latino students seem to have a tough time writing in their scholarly voice. Why? This is because in our culture we are taught not to brag or boast about our accomplishments. However, we must break through this mindset in order to articulate how our academic and intellectual abilities are closely aligned or superior to the candidates sought at competitive universities.

What does "scholarly" writing look like? Here is an example of a student who chose to use scientific terms to demonstrate her intellectual curiosity:

During my internship at UC San Diego, I had the opportunity to sit in on a lecture by world-renowned scientist Dr. V.S. Ramachandran. Dr. Ramachandran discussed his studies in behavioral neurology and cognitive neuroscience. One of the most fascinating of these areas was his work in neural mechanisms and underlying human perception — specifically, his work on "phantom limbs." This phenomena occurs when a patient who has had either a limb amputated or is paralyzed still perceives sensation in the area of their amputated or paralyzed limb.

For example, Dr. Ramachandran described how his patients complained their phantom limb was painful because it was twisted in a strange way, and they could not adjust or alter its position. Dr. Ramachandran's amazing discovery was very simple. He asked patients to look in a mirror focusing on their normal, functioning, limb. He would have them move that functioning limb while staring into the mirror — making it appear as if their phantom limb was moving normally.

The fact our brain can perceive sensation without a physical stimuli or a physical presence is perplexing. However, the fact visual stimuli without physical stimuli can affect the somatosensory cortex, is even more perplexing. I wish to do research in this area to learn whether there exists a correlation between patients

who have a Phantom limb and a deficiency or excess of a specific neurotransmit-
ter in the area of amputation or in the somatosensory cortex. Phenomena like this
is precisely why the field of neuroscience is so engaging to me.

In this example, Gabriella spoke in her scholarly voice. She did not simply say, "I like the topic of neuroscience and I learned about this cool thing called Phantom Limb Theory." Instead, she spoke in scientific terms, demonstrating her intellectual curiosity. She didn't assume her audience wouldn't understand the complex phenomenon she was describing.

For another great example demonstrating the "Intellectual" component, see Chapter 13, *Supplemental Essays*.

Narrative. Narrative can be defined in several ways, depending on the context. In this context, we are speaking of the tense, form, or mode in which the author speaks. It is the grammatical first-person. The point of view of your essay will be referred to as the first person narrative. You will explicitly refer to yourself using words and phrases involving "I" (referred to as the first person singular) and/or "we."

My students tell me they feel more comfortable speaking in third-person because of the formal nature of the college essay. They were also schooled by their English teachers that it is not appropriate to speak in first person. When their draft essays hit my desk, they are often laden with "One might say" or "One should focus on one's ability to . . ." However, recall in Chapter 2 "*What is the Personal Statement?*" the essay is your way to connect personally with the admissions reader. It makes sense, then, to write in first person narrative.

In addition to speaking in first-person, you also need to speak in your authentic voice. It is obvious when a student tosses in words that clearly came straight from a thesaurus. For example, what if I said, "My acquaintances are multifarious, enthralling, and engrossing." This sounds forced, awkward, and phony. It would be better to say, "I have an interesting and diverse group of friends." Your goal is not to impress the admissions reader with sophisticated words. Your goal is to *clearly* communicate your ideas and thoughts.

> *"But Quetzal Mama, in the "I" for "Intellectual,*
> *you just told us to write in our Scholarly Voice.*
> *What's the difference between sophisticated words*
> *and a scholarly voice?"*

Using a Scholarly Voice doesn't mean using fancy words. It means your writing should demonstrate intellectual curiosity and depth. This can be demonstrated by conveying critical thinking and analysis. Or, it can be demonstrated by appropriately citing a technical term. For example, in the student's essay regarding Phantom Limb Theory, she included scientific terms such as *neurotransmitter* and *somatosensory cortex*.

Having said that, you may now be wondering:

- Will my essay appear unsophisticated if I do not use flowery language?
- Will the admissions reader assume I do not possess an extensive vocabulary?
- Will my essay lack extra "flavor" if I replace highly descriptive words with basic words?

- What if I *really do* talk like that? I am quite verbose and accustomed to writing in this fashion.

The answer to the first three questions above is, "No." Let's address each question separately.

First, the sophistication of your essay will be conveyed through various essay components. It may be through the complex and interesting theme you have chosen, the manner in which you cleverly devise your thesis, the way you demonstrate your critical thinking skills, or the precise way you articulate important details.

Second, the admissions reader will make assumptions about your extensive vocabulary (or lack thereof) from details derived from your overall profile. For example, experienced high school writers are easily identified through many activities such as: placing first in the essay portion of the Academic Decathlon, achieving an A grade in AP or IB English, holding the position of Editor for the school newspaper, or writing displayed within your cyber profile. *Learn about the Cyber Profile in Chapter 11, "Social Netiquette" Flight of the Quetzal Mama.*

Last, the "flavor" expressed in your essay will not be limited to sophisticated words. Instead, be clear and concise in the selection of your words for a stronger essay. The "flavor" will come through by selecting the appropriate details in which you focus. See Chapter 6, *"The Personal Statement is Like a Taco de Carne Asada."*

The fourth question is a valid one. What if you *do really* talk like that? There are some exceptional high school students who are crafty writers with extensive vocabularies. How do you know if you meet these criteria? Does your Honors or AP/IB teacher tell you this? Do words glide off your keyboard, with ease and clarity? Have you received awards for your writing? Will you be pursuing a career as a writer? Or, are you just a naturally gifted writer? If you answered, "Yes" to these questions, then you may wish to dial up the vocabulary within your essay.

Compelling Introduction. I tell my students that having a compelling introduction is like fishing. You have to hook your bait and cast your reel to "catch" the reader's attention. In my practice, I recommend three types of "hooks" for greatest appeal. These hooks include using a quote, storytelling, or answering a question. Let's talk about using a quote.

You can find several compelling quotes online through a simple search. However, be careful to avoid using cliché and commonly used quotes. For example, you may consider using one of the following powerful quotes by famous Latinos:

"My mother fought hard for civil rights so that instead of a mop, I could hold this microphone." **—Julián Castro**

"Until we get equality in education, we won't have an equal society." **— Sonia Sotomayor**

"The end of all education should surely be service to others." **—César Chavez**

"Pride and roots are what it is. It definitely does not mean separation or nationalism in the sense that we want to go back to Mexico." **— Dolores Huerta**

"Every day, everything I do -- it doesn't matter if I was a welder or when I was a tomato picker -- I gave it my best." — **Dr. Alfredo Quiñones-Hinojosa**

One of my students — an aspiring entrepreneur, used the following quotation for effect in her introductory paragraph:

> *"I've always said that the better off you are, the more responsibility you have for helping others." This quote is by an individual with whom many Americans are not familiar, yet for two consecutive years he has held the title of being the world's wealthiest person: Carlos Slim Helú. While I truly admire Carlos Slim Helu's business mind, theories, and his practical and highly effective business management principles, it is his philosophical ideals that have most inspired me.*

A clever way to incorporate a quote, and demonstrate your passion for a particular subject matter, is to quote from an industry source, newspaper headline, or book. For example, one of my students applying to a competitive business program included this reference:

> *When I read the New York Times article, "How Chicago's Housing Crisis Ignited a New Form of Activism," I was inspired. As a business major, this article . . .*

In this example, the student responded to the quote by providing his personal analysis of the housing crisis. This was a brilliant way to demonstrate to the admissions readers that he was both passionate and knowledgeable about his major (business).

Another "hook" or strategy for a compelling introduction is to tell a story. Fortunately, we Latinos have many interesting stories! The beauty of storytelling is that it is *your* story — not someone else's story. You are the best person to write your story because only you know the details, the subtle nuances, and the chronology of events for your story. So what does storytelling look like? Here is an example:

> *Standing in the women's restroom at Stanford University Hospital, I laughed at the image of the girl staring back at me. I couldn't believe where I was and how far I had come from the agricultural valley of my small town of Tracy. The image I saw was a young Latina dressed in blue surgical scrubs with big brown eyes brimming with optimism. I felt proud as I clipped on my official Stanford badge, one that all the other doctors wear, and placed my cotton blue surgical cap on my head. In that moment I felt thankful and humbled I had been given a once-in-a-lifetime opportunity to pursue my passion: neuroscience. This was my first day as an intern in the Neurodiagnostics Lab at Stanford University Hospital. I had just been instructed to change into a pair of scrubs so I could make my first trip to the operating room. After staring in the mirror for a few more seconds, I grabbed my clothes, gave thanks to La Virgin de Guadalupe, took a deep breath, and stepped out of the restroom a new person. In those few seconds of seeing myself in scrubs, I knew that all of my preparation had led me to this point.*

In this example, this student told the story of her first day of a summer internship. Through descriptive detail, we can almost "feel" her excitement and imagine ourselves standing in that bathroom. It is quite interesting that this student chose the bathroom — of all places, as the backdrop for her story. Ironically, this detail is quite effective, and invokes an inspirational feeling.

Ask a Question. Asking a question is another clever way to capture your reader. For example, you present a rhetorical question, followed by your interpretation/response to the question:

> *Why is it that most Americans can pronounce words like 'croissant' and 'cabernet savignon' with ease, perfectly mimicking the French intonation of CWAH-SON, yet intentionally mispronouncing Spanish words like jalapeno or quesadilla?*

Or, you can refer to a commonly asked question, followed by your unique interpretation and response to the question:

> *Many have wondered why we celebrate Cinco de Mayo in the United States, while this is only celebrated regionally in México. As a Chicano Studies major, my theory is informed by . . .*

Or simply present a question and then respond to it:

> *Was I surprised when I read the article, "Unequal Burden: Income and Racial Disparities in Subprime Lending in America"? No, I was not. As a Finance major, my perspective has been informed by . . .*

How about using a silly question to pique interest? For example, "Did you know the Blue-footed booby does a courtship dance to attract his female partner?" Explain why this humorous question relates to you.

You can see that any of the three techniques we discussed is an effective strategy to capture our reader's attention. Whether we select a quote, tell a story, or ask a question, we have a proven strategy to grab our reader's interest.

Answer the Prompt. This may be the most difficult part of the essay for many students. When students read a prompt, they sometimes focus on essay components that are irrelevant within the early stages of writing. For example, they are seeking a clever theme or how to sound intellectual. Instead, they should focus on the very basic task of answering the prompt. The prompt is simply a question the student must answer. To best illustrate how a student might get off track and fail to answer the prompt, enjoy this movie reference.

> **"This is where you live. Right here.**
> **You live right here, okay. This is home."**
> **—From *Hitch* by Columbia Pictures**

One of my favorite films is *Hitch* by Columbia Pictures. My favorite scene is where Albert Brennaman, Kevin James' character, demonstrates his dance moves to Alex 'Hitch' Hitchens, Will Smith's character. Brennaman tells Hitch that he is not at all worried about his dance moves. He says, "Dancing is the one thing I'm not worried about. Trust me." He confidently demonstrates his moves such as "rolling the dough," "making a pizza," "doing the Q-tip," and "throwing it away." After he finishes, Hitch slaps him and says, "Don't *ever* do that again!"

I love this dance scene because it reminds me of some of the students I've coached through the years. Instead of focusing on the prompt, answering the basic question(s), structuring the essay in a logical manner, and solidifying key points, some of my students are all over the page, literally! They are like Albert Brennaman — dancing around the prompt without answering it. What am I talking about? Here is an example.

Fernando provided this response to the Common Application prompt: <u>Discuss some issue of personal, local, national, or international concern and its importance to you.</u>

> *We human beings can contribute to the sea of knowledge our ancestors have left us as we progress and transcend global issues together as a society. We must be diligent in permeating the orifice of society's ills and hindering its progress. Only through nurturing, sustaining, and satiating global issues will we immobilize factors detrimental to our success.*

Huh? Fernando's response is vague and confusing. We have no idea what he is saying, or where he is going. His introduction would have been much more effective had he used clear language, and avoided the thesaurus. Most importantly, he should have focused on answering the prompt succinctly. How did Fernando fix this? I recommended that Fernando choose a concise introductory paragraph that naturally led to his main point — answering the prompt. Here is Fernando's edited response:

> *Standing in a crowded room of 168 students, we stood — holding candles and anxiously awaiting the announcement. The work, sweat, and energy we put into our campaign culminated with a single stoke of the pen. It was October 8, 2011, and California Governor Jerry Brown had just signed the California Dream Act. This political issue is of personal interest and significant importance to me, and has been a catalyst in solidifying my desire to major in political science as an undergraduate.*

Want to keep reading? Yes, you do. Fernando has piqued our interest and we want to know more. He precisely answered the prompt, and in subsequent paragraphs he discussed how this political issue impacted his perspective. In the second and third paragraphs, Fernando provided concrete examples of his academic and civic-related activities such as his volunteer service at the Coalition for Humane Immigrant Rights of Los Angeles (CHIRLA). Fernando's compelling story convinced the admission reader that he is passionate about politics, is a leader in his field, is concerned about his community, and will make a significant contribution to a selective college campus.

Speak to Audience. In the context of college essays, the language of politics is critical. More so than other mediums, what you say and to whom has critical significance. In Chapter 2, *Overview of the Personal Statement*, I've outlined the makeup of those individuals reading your essays.

Know this: Words are *not* neutral and your essay is *not* apolitical. Be mindful of the politics that go into your essay theme, tone, and language, and how it impacts (positively or negatively) your overall profile.

Consider the following audiences. Reader A is a life-long member of the Conservative Caucus, whose tagline is "Uncompromising Defenders of American Liberty Since 1974." Reader B serves on the Board of the National Council of La Raza, the largest national Hispanic civil rights and advocacy organization in the United States. Considering the two readers, which terms might be positively or negatively received?

Latino	versus	Hispanic
Undocumented Student	versus	Illegal Alien
Affirmative Action	versus	Reverse Discrimination
Pro Choice	versus	Pro Life

Since we cannot know the political affiliation or religious views of our reader, it is unwise to write about such a polarizing topic. However, although we cannot predict which admissions representative will read your particular essay, there are some safe assumptions you should make.

First, assume that the individual reading your essay is a human being, and not a robot. I say this jokingly to stress a point. Human beings are sensitive people with personal biases, political ideologies, and membership to a specific socio-economic and racial/ethnic group. As humans, we make judgments — whether consciously or subconsciously, as to the merit of an applicant's essay.

I'm not suggesting admission readers only praise student writing that emulates their political position and ideology. I'm saying *cuídate*. Err on the side of cautiously selecting your content and language.

Second, assume there will be many types of folks reading your essay including recent college graduates, tenured department faculty, and full-time employees within the admissions staff.

Knowing to whom you are speaking helps you to modify and tailor your style appropriately. Admissions personnel take their jobs seriously. As such, they expect students will project an appropriate level of maturity and professionalism within the essay. Here are a few tips to help you speak to your audience:

1. Include technical references to convey your passion and intellectual abilities concerning your intended major;
2. Signify respect to your audience by avoiding cheesy humor, informality, or inappropriate language.

Authenticity. Specifically, we are speaking about Cultural Authenticity. My definition of Cultural Authenticity within a college essay follows:

> *Cultural Authenticity refers to the quality a student possesses that represents positive, strong, and consistent affiliation within a cultural group. This quality is based on authentic life experiences within the culture and examples may include religion, politics, language, traditions, and historical knowledge.*
> *—Quetzal Mama*

Why does Cultural Authenticity matter in college admissions? It matters because colleges seek to diversify their incoming freshman class with students who bring a unique set of experiences, insight, and ideas into their classrooms.

Imagine the dialogue, learning experiences, and climate at a campus where *everyone* looked, sounded, thought, and spoke the same. Colleges understand that diversity enhances their campus in positive ways. For this reason, all things being equal (academic qualifications), the student who can bring diversity to a campus will shine.

Unfortunately, many high school students undervalue or disregard the significance of Cultural Authenticity in their Personal Statement. They mistakenly believe that checking a box ("Please indicate how you identify yourself") on the college application confirms their "authenticity." This is not sufficient as it does not inform the college as to the student's life experiences, perspectives, nor the diversity the student would bring to their campus. There are subtle and significant differences between a student merely born into a race/ethnic group, and a student who has authentically "lived" this experience.

Fortunately for admissions readers, they can easily detect which students demonstrate cultural authenticity, versus those who are merely "box checkers." One way to discern this information is within the content of their Personal Statement.

Let's look at one of the current Common Application prompts that may help leverage cultural authenticity. Vanessa chose Prompt No. 1:

> *Some students have a background or story that is so central to their identity that they believe their application would be incomplete without it. If this sounds like you, then please share your story.*

This prompt is a perfect segue to demonstrate cultural authenticity. Vanessa has a multitude of avenues to exemplify cultural authenticity. She might share a story about her experiences growing up in a particular geographic area, her experiences as a member of a particular ethnic group, or involvement with a particular political organization.

The key is to identify the background or story, and then focus on how this experience(s) has shaped the student's perspective. Specifically, it is the way in which the event, story, or experience informs and guides the student's thinking process, attitude, philosophy, and interactions with his or her world that truly exemplifies cultural authenticity.

Some of the techniques I recommend students employ when articulating cultural authenticity is to include terms and concepts that demonstrate the degree of their knowledge concerning the topic. Examples might include language, visual imagery, or technical details. The following is such an example:

> *As we drive into Tijuana, I immediately inhale the heavenly smell of fried lengua and cesos. My eyes scan the perpetual grey skies, Taqueros on every street corner, and Tejuino vendors peddling their elixirs. Dogs and children run through the streets, ignoring the stench of raw sewage. As we drive up the unpaved, muddy streets toward the Barrio of Los Altos, I am on my way to my second home. Passing by shacks and crude cement structures, these are the homes of our neighbors. I have returned to this barrio nearly every year since I was an infant. While this experience may sound unappealing to some, this is a joyous experience for me. I am proud of this part of my background as it has shaped my perspective in life, and has offered me a unique way of viewing the world.*

After presenting a vivid introduction, Vanessa will use subsequent paragraphs to describe how this experience shaped her view of the world and influenced her decision to study Public Health. Within the first couple of sentences Vanessa refers to *"lengua"* and *"cesos"* (tongue and brains), *"Taqueros"* (taco vendors) and *"Tejuino"* (a fermented corn drink). In recalling these concepts and using her native language (Spanish) to describe them, Vanessa conveys authenticity. How else could Vanessa recall such vivid imagery unless she genuinely experienced this?

The introductory paragraph above is an exaggerated example. I intentionally selected language to illustrate my point in a direct and obvious way. However, I caution students against including gratuitous language purely for effect. For example, saying that, *"Dogs and children run through the streets"* could unintentionally connote that the children in Tijuana are like animals — a negative connotation. This may be counterproductive if the student does not consider how their approach may inadvertently perpetuate negative stereotypes.

Another avenue to express cultural authenticity is through traditions and ritual. Some of my students have written eloquent essays regarding the spiritual impact of the *la posada*, lighting candles to honor *Nuestra Señora de Guadalupe*, making *cascarones* during *Pascua*, or decorating *calaveras* for *Día de Los Muertos*. Still others have described their cultural authenticity through the arts. These students highlighted their performance in a *mariachi* group, *ballet folklorico* troupe, *teatro*, or described how they decorated a float for a *Cinco de Mayo* celebration.

Sometimes cultural authenticity is best exemplified in subtle, not obvious ways. For example, the introduction might include *un dicho*; an expression by a family member; or a quote by an influential Latino scholar, philosopher, historian, or politician. All of these openers are ideal expressions demonstrating cultural authenticity. Here is an example:

> *Growing up, mi abuelito used to always tell me, "Si vas a hacer algo, hazlo bien." Being a rambunctious child, I would nod my head quickly and reply, "Si, lo entiendo." As a young child I did not fully appreciate his cautionary advice, but I recognized the sincerity and forthright manner in which he said it. As I grew older and became more diligent in my academic studies, I slowly began to appreciate the wisdom behind his words . . .*

Keep in mind that cultural authenticity is not something that suddenly emerges during the senior year of high school! It will be clear to an admissions officer those students who were not involved in activities throughout high school, but attempt to pad their profile at the last moment. Consistency is an important factor.

In summary, students who wish to speak effectively to cultural authenticity within their Personal Statement should consider the following:

1. Merely saying you are culturally authentic is not enough. Prove it. Provide clear examples within your essay.

2. Identify the context or situation, and then focus on how this experience has shaped your perspective.

3. Use terms, concepts, and technical details to describe your authenticity.

4. Examples of cultural authenticity do not need to be blatant or obvious. Sometimes the best examples are those that are subtle.

5. Carefully balance the use of terms with political and cultural sensitivity; avoid perpetuating negative stereotypes.

6. Don't trivialize the concept of cultural authenticity by projecting a simplistic view of this concept. Instead, describe in detail the depth and complexity of your understanding.

7. Cultural authenticity can include involvement in a politically, ethnically, and culturally affiliated group.

8. Consistency is key to demonstrating cultural authenticity. Don't wait until your senior year of high school to join a cultural group. A True pattern will emerge from viewing your college application.

Recap of TIN CASA
Use the TIN CASA rubic *after* composing your draft essay.
Use this rubric as a way to "check" your content.

"T" Tone
Tone shouldn't be too formal or informal, but in the middle.
Your goal is uplifting, inspirational, and optimistic.

"I" Intellectual
Demonstrate your intellectual depth and curiosity.

"N" Narrative
The story is about you. Write it in First Person narrative.

"C" Compelling Introduction
Use one of three hooks to grab your reader's attention including
using a quote, storytelling, or answering a question.

"A" Answer the Prompt
Don't overlook the obvious. Stay focused and answer the prompt.

"S" Speak to Your Audience

Admission readers are not robots. College essays are not apolitical. Words are not neutral. Cautiously address your audience.

"A" Authenticity (Cultural)

Convey cultural authenticity by referring to positive life experiences within a cultural group. This can be achieved through references in religion, politics, language, traditions, and/or historical knowledge.

Tip!

If you use culturally authentic language within your essay, make sure to translate the word or phrase into English.
For example:

Growing up, mi abuelito used to always tell me, "Si vas a hacer algo, hazlo bien" ("If you're going to do something, do it well"). Being a rambunctious child, I would nod my head quickly and reply, "Si, lo entiendo" ("Yes, I understand").

Part Three

Overarching Themes

The *Ganas* Principle

Leadership – A Misnomer

The S/hero's Journey

8

The Ganas Principle

"'Ganas = desire + determination + discipline'
and that's all we need to learn!"
—Jaime Escalante

The *Ganas* Principle. I coined this principle after conducting numerous essay writing workshops. As I was articulating to my students the basic essence of what they should capture, it came to me: *Ganas*.

So, let's talk about *ganas*. I love this term because nearly all Latinos know what I mean when I say *ganas*. Even the very young students attending my workshops will raise their hands when I ask, "What does *ganas* mean?" They often say it means passion, grit, desire, determination, and mostly, "having the guts" to do something. We all know students who have *ganas*. They are students who push themselves toward excellence, often defying obstacles.

These superior qualities are especially appealing from an admissions perspective. They are part of the "proof" admissions staff seek in prospective candidates. How so? Three reasons.

One – admissions folks know that students who display certain predispositions, like resiliency and determination, have greater odds of academic success. And, they know what researchers know – that this attitude, when measured against other factors for success like grade point average, matters *most*.

Two – If you can survive and thrive academically despite the limiting conditions addressed in your application or essay, then imagine your academic contribution at a campus that provides exceptional resources for student success.

Three – Possibly the most important reason universities seek students with *ganas* is that they know this characteristic will not vanish once their selected undergraduate student commences with his/her studies. They know the spirit of *ganas* is what makes the future leaders of the business world, political arena, and scientific community.

In other words, students who demonstrate *ganas* will likely bring these skills and mindset with them as they pursue their academic studies, as well as into future business and leadership endeavors.

Do you have *ganas*? And, if you have *ganas*, how do you convey this to the admissions reader? Let's talk about how your personal narrative might convey *ganas*. We don't have space in this chapter to cover every possible scenario, so we'll focus on three examples to convey *ganas*: overcoming obstacles, community service, and discipline related activities.

Overcoming Obstacles. The students I coach have overcome many, many obstacles. You may also identify with some or many of these obstacles, including attending low resourced high schools — sometimes without comprehensive AP or IB programs — lack of high school counselling services, many with a 800:1 counselor/student ratio, lack of tailored and individualized college-going information, lack of financial aid knowledge, ineffective high school intervention programs, anti-social messaging regarding intellectual or cultural inferiority, and lack of socio-cultural capital to navigate the selective college process. In addition to these obstacles, let's add being low-income, first generation college students, English Language Learners, and being undocumented.

If you have overcome just one, some, or several of the obstacles listed above, and are *still* on your pathway to college, then by default — you have *ganas*! Now, your challenge is to write about how you overcame these difficulties through determination and resilience.

But, it's not just about surviving obstacles. The key to convey *ganas* in your essay is to demonstrate *how* you maneuvered through the obstacle. It is the *spirit* of how you maneuvered that demonstrates *ganas*. Therefore, we want to articulate the personal characteristics that exemplify *ganas* such as resilience, initiative, persistence, and drive.

For example, saying that your high school does not have an AP or IB program is not enough. You must *describe* what you did (action) in response to the challenge, and what mental perspective or attitude (mindset) moved you to take that action. To illustrate what I'm talking about, in this next essay I've highlighted the phrases that illustrate how the student conveyed *ganas*:

> *When I enrolled as a freshman at Barack Obama High School, I learned our school did not have an AP program. I was disappointed for two reasons. It meant I would miss out on four years of a rigorous and intellectually challenging curriculum. It also meant that as a senior, I would have a tough time demonstrating to colleges that I was as qualified and capable as other applicants.*
>
> *Because* **I had researched the profile of students** *admitted to the colleges I was considering, I learned that competitive students had taken at least five or six AP courses by the time they applied. Therefore, my challenge was to* **identify a solution** *to my challenge.* **I solved this challenge by doing three things.**
>
> *First, I found online college courses I could enroll and participate throughout the school year. Second, I found local Community Colleges that offered Saturday session, intersession, and hybrid courses. Finally, I obtained permission from our Registrar so that I could earn high school credits for these courses, and have my performance noted on my official transcript.*

*Having **strategized** ways to **overcome** our school's lack of an AP pro-*
*gram helped me **accomplish many goals**. I was able to receive a college*
level understanding of American History, Calculus and Discrete Mathematics,
Biology, English Literature, and Philosophy. I was also introduced to the rigor
of college level coursework as a preparation for my undergraduate studies. But,
*most importantly, I learned that **maintaining an optimistic and***
***determined mindset** is especially important. This mindset helped me*
***focus on finding a solution**, rather than accepting limitations.*

You can see that the student not only responded to the obstacle, but also helped the reader understand how he approached his challenge. He nailed his essay by conveying his mindset of initiative, persistence, and optimism. He's a go-getter and he has *ganas*!

Community Service. Community Service is another example of how you might exemplify *ganas*. I'm defining service as anything you do in service to others — whether it occurs on campus, in your local community, or as an ambassador within the larger community.

For example, did you create a club at your high school that has a community service focus? How about designing a workshop for elementary students in your local community? Perhaps you hosted a bake sale to fundraise for your county's child abuse shelter? Or, maybe you are the community service chairperson for your campus MEChA organization?

In this community service context, *ganas* is not conveyed simply through the formation or your involvement in a club or service project. It is through the way in which you describe the actions you took *and* by describing the motivating factor(s) or characteristics that prompted you to take these actions. Why? Because admissions folks know that students who have *ganas*, do not accept mediocrity or the status quo. They shake things up, and they make things happen. And, they often do these things because they are motivated and inspired by a higher power. What might this look like in Personal Statement? Here is an example:

> As César Chávez said, "The end of all education should surely be service to others." Having been raised in a migrant farm camp, his words are especially important to me. I came to the United States when I was eight years old. Living in a migrant camp, **I struggled** to learn English. **I challenged myself** by taking ESL courses at a local community organization, eventually becoming fluent at the age of 12. As I grew older, and looked around my camp, I saw other young children struggling to learn English. It was at that time I **felt the spirit** of César Chávez' **vision for service.**
>
> Through his inspiration, I began volunteering within my community. I was **determined** to help others by serving as a volunteer English tutor. **I choose to volunteer my time** with other migrant kids because I understand the obstacles and barriers they face — the same barriers and obstacles I faced. They want to learn English to be successful, but there are factors that make it challenging for them. For example, they must return to Mexico with their families for four or five months each year, when the seasonal crops end. This means our tutoring sessions are **limited, but very important.**
>
> **I am determined** to help them succeed academically so they can change their future and have the same opportunities I've had. My career goal is to become a Clinical Psychologist. I intend to pursue this field so that I can counsel migrant youth who have experienced challenging life situations. As an aspiring psychologist, César Chavez' words **inspire me** to pursue higher education. His words remind me that my influence as a future psychologist will serve those

who are most in need of my service. These encouraging words will help me to stay **focused and diligent** *in my pursuit of higher education.*

This example demonstrates this student's initiative ("I choose to volunteer my time") and determination to accomplish her educational goals. She tells us where her inspiration comes from, and how this helps her remain "focused and diligent." In this instance, the student is motivated and inspired to serve by a higher power. This power gives her the strength and *ganas* to achieve her goals!

Discipline-Related Activities. Demonstrating *ganas* through discipline-related activities accomplishes two things. It communicates your passion (*ganas*) for your chosen major, and it demonstrates your motivation (*ganas*) to succeed as a college student.

Let's say that you intend to major in Political Science. To demonstrate *ganas* in this context you will need to articulate your passion for Political Science and provide examples of how your passion resulted in specific outcomes. What would this look like in a Personal Statement? Here is an example:

My interest in politics began at a very early age. It was spring of 2006 — when students were walking out of class and off campus in protest to immigration reform legislation. At my middle school, I **convinced my peers** *that we could stage a peaceful and informative demonstration on campus, versus walking out. I met with my Principal,* **proposed the idea,** *and explained how the demonstration would benefit our student body. My Principal granted permission to* **host the demonstration,** *but it would not be without conflict. While me and my two friends rapidly collected 500 signatures from fellow students in* *support of an immigration reform bill, we could sense tension. Just outside of the auditorium were armed police officers, patrol cars, truancy officers, and full security. Even our Superintendent made an appearance.*

Although the signatures were only symbolic, I carefully took the tattered sheets of paper to my local Post Office and mailed them to Senator Diane Feinstein and the late Senator Edward "Ted" Kennedy. This was my introduction into the world of politics and it was exciting.

*Having tasted a bit of political ideology in middle school, I was **determined to take every political science course offered** at my high school. Enrolling in AP Comparative Government & Politics, AP US Government & Politics, AP World History, and AP Microeconomics, helped me develop a keen sense of the fascinating complexities that govern the world of politics.*

*However, it was not until I attended the Chicano Latino Youth **Leadership Project** in Sacramento, California, that I gained a broader view concerning Latino politics. Here I learned first-hand about the legislative process through a mock hearing, as well as interacting with state legislators and legislative staff. The following year I participated in the LegiSchool Project's Real World Civics **Summer Internship** program. In this five week internship program I was exposed to all branches of state government and it solidified my desire to pursue Political Science as an undergraduate.*

From my middle school days, throughout three years of AP History curriculum, to participating in a summer conference and a legislative internship, I am now ready to embark on another exciting journey in politics. This time, it will be in a university classroom, with other scholars, dissecting domestic and international political systems.

In the example above, we see how the student's passion for political science grew and evolved. The way she details her seven year journey experiencing the world of politics indicates incredible persistence, diligence, and tenacity. Clearly, she has *ganas*! She nailed it.

Recap

Ganas is defined as personal characteristics, traits, or an essence exemplified as initiative, persistence, resilience, grit, diligence, and drive.

Ganas also means "having the guts" to do something. Students with *ganas* shake things up, and get things done!

Conveying *ganas* in a Personal Statement does two things: It demonstrates you have the internal drive and motivation to achieve your goals. It demonstrates you are passionate about a specific discipline.

The key to convey *ganas* in your essay is to demonstrate *how* you maneuvered through an obstacle or experience.

It is not the event, obstacle, or experience that conveys *ganas*. Rather, it is the *spirit* of how you maneuvered that demonstrates *ganas*.

9

Leadership - A Misnomer

The goal of this chapter is to help students understand how the traditional definition of "leadership" can be very misleading in an admissions context.

To illustrate my point, let's look at Dictionary.com's definition of the term, "leadership." It is defined as, "The position or function of a leader, a person who directs or guides a group." This definition indicates there is a lone individual, whose leadership ability is achieved by guiding others in a group setting.

Now, let's look at the definition of "Misnomer." It is defined as, "A word or term that suggests a meaning that is known to be wrong. A misnomer may also be a word that is used incorrectly or misleadingly."

I bring these two concepts together to explain how the traditional term "leadership" is often misleading for Latino students. I label this term a "misnomer" because "leadership" is often perceived incorrectly by students, misleading them to believe they are *not* leaders based on a traditional definition.

The way in which Latino students misunderstand the concept of leadership became apparent to me one Saturday afternoon during a coaching session with a brilliant student named Jesús. Jesús came to me, with his parents, eager to learn how he might increase his chances of getting into two dream schools: Stanford University and UCLA.

After discussing how he should focus on conveying leadership qualities, Jesús looked somewhat defeated and said, "I understand why leadership is important. But, I'm a shy person. I don't feel comfortable in a leadership role, so I am not a leader. I won't get into Stanford or UCLA."

Jesús' honest assessment of his personality really threw me. I knew exactly what he meant. I also knew I neglected to properly define leadership qualities; and, therefore, we were not talking about the same concept. I neglected to tell Jesús that the term, "leadership" is a misnomer, that leadership qualities are not limited to being extroverted, aggressive, and outwardly vocal.

I was baffled by Jesús' assessment because I saw him as an authentic leader. Yes, he was quiet and shy. However, he possessed internal leadership qualities that he overlooked. For example, he was voted "Most Inspirational Player" by his cross country team. He also demonstrated leadership by taking initiative to design an after school program for fourth graders.

Furthermore, Jesús demonstrated the leadership quality of resilience by enrolling in local community college courses because his small, charter high school did not offer AP or IB curriculum. Unfortunately, Jesús made the mistake many students make — viewing leadership through a very narrow lens. He could not see how his personal characteristics of initiative and resilience qualified him as a leader.

Many students, like Jesús, *mistakenly* equate "leadership" ability with iconic titles such as Class President, or Captain of the Speech & Debate Team. However, the leadership qualities that admissions folks seek are not confined to these limited roles. Often, the most effective and successful leaders demonstrate a soft-spoken or "quiet" leadership. What qualifies as a "leader" may be defined by many unique characteristics, such as:

- Inability/refusal to accept mediocrity
- Perseverance
- Passion
- Focus

- Vision
- Stick-to-itiveness
- Perfection in pursuit of a particular endeavor
- Being a change agent — impacting change in your community

As you can see from these definitions, a student does not necessarily have to be vocal or extroverted. A quiet and non-vocal person can hold these traits. You can also see from the above bulleted points that the concept and characteristics of leadership and *ganas* are complimentary. See Chapter 8, The *Ganas* Principle.

Back to Jesús. My task at hand was to convince Jesús that he possessed leadership skills. Instead of telling him, I directed him to the UCLA admissions site so that he could read the personal qualities they seek in an applicant:

> **Personal qualities of the applicant,** *including leadership ability, character, motivation, tenacity, initiative, originality, creativity, intellectual independence, responsibility, insight, maturity, and demonstrated concern for others and for the community. These qualities may not be reflected in traditional measures of academic achievement. They may be found elsewhere in the application and judged by the reader as positive indicators of the student's ability to succeed at UCLA and beyond.*

If you read UCLA's description carefully, you will notice that while leadership ability is listed first, other characteristics listed are also indicative of leadership.

What does this mean for you? It means you should think beyond cliché or "traditional" definitions of leadership. Instead, consider what you do in your home, neighborhood, high school campus, local community, or the larger community, that demonstrates leadership. Look past titles, and consider your personal strengths and characteristics. Often these personal qualities are the best indicator of leadership.

What Do Admissions Experts Say About "Leadership"

Rather than describing my own theories regarding how to convey "Leadership," I decided to go straight to the source! Just for the students reading this book, I interviewed college admissions directors from the top universities in the US and asked them to define *their version* of authentic "leadership." As you will see below, there are many non-traditional definitions of what it means to be a "leader" from an admissions perspective.

So, let's hear directly from Directors of Admission from our nation's top universities regarding their perception of "Leadership":

Leadership may certainly be through traditional avenues such as elected leadership. However, it can also be demonstrated within a community space such as supporting after school programs for younger children, teaching in a religious institution, addressing environmental conservation, fundraising for a club or to fund summer research, or tutoring classmates in areas of academic strength. We truly value the spaces where the student is in a position of responsibility for others, or where they have taken the initiative to serve.

— Anne M. De Luca, Ph.D.
Associate Vice Chancellor, Admissions & Enrollment
University of California Berkeley

I think the term leadership becomes very confusing. It really has to do with whether someone makes things happen — whether for themselves or for their community. It is more useful to ask students, "What type of contribution do you make toward your success and other's success?

— Dr. Elizabeth Hart
Director of Multicultural Recruitment
Brown University

There are different types of leaders. We see many Latino applicants who are from low-income families, and whose parents work night shifts. This means the high school student is responsible for managing their younger siblings — assisting them with homework and school projects, cooking their meals, and handling many chores. In assuming the role of "parent" they are using the same management skills we seek. Taking on the role of a surrogate parent is often far more challenging than being an officer of a high school club. We hope students will not overlook this important skill set.

— Abraham Lopez
Admissions Officer
University of California, Merced

The qualities that make a good leader are not always obvious. They may be more subtle. Oftentimes the best leaders are quiet leaders, who do not desire the limelight and who may not be comfortable being the center of attention. Great leaders know how to listen and are adept at understanding the needs of those around them; they demonstrate initiative in helping others, and they are able to inspire people through their determination, their words, and their actions. Any given high school has only one Student Body President at a time. However, there are many unelected student–leaders who are able to make a difference at their schools, in their church communities, in their neighborhoods, and within their families.

— Monica Hernandez
Assistant Director of Undergraduate Admissions
University of Notre Dame

Recap
The term "leader" is often misleading for Latino students.
Think beyond traditional definitions of leadership.
Consider ways that you demonstrate leadership within your home,
local community, or through your academic studies.

10

The S/hero's Journey

A highly effective Personal Statement strategy can be found in a timeless, universal, storytelling theme known as the "Hero's Journey." I've updated the pronoun to make it gender neutral. You will recognize this theme from your AP English course — often called the "Hero's Quest" or the "Hero's Journey." It is one of the most effective storytelling themes and it can be found in literary works across millennia and across nearly all cultures.

In a nutshell, the structure goes like this: The S/hero is identified as being remarkable, special, or gifted in some aspect. The S/hero receives a "call to adventure," and with some type of supernatural assistance, embarks on a journey to another dimension. During this adventure, the S/hero will encounter many trials and tribulations, will redeem him/herself, and will eventually emerges as a S/hero.

Here's a S/hero's Journey you may recall. In *Popol Vuh: The Sacred Book of the Ancient Quiché Maya*, the hero twins *Hunahpú* and *Xbalanque* descend into *Xibalba* (the underworld), to defeat the Lords of *Xibalba* in a ballgame. Throughout their journey, they encountered many trials including the House of Gloom, House of Knives, House of Cold, House of Jaguars, House of Fire, and House of Bats. The twins emerged triumphant. One became the Sun, and the other became the Moon.

The S/hero's Journey is also a common theme that works with most of my students. To see what I mean, let's replace the players and situations with a student I will call "Meysel."

Our student Meysel was summoned by a supernatural force, her *abuelita*! Her grandmother identified her potential and talents and challenged her to descend into the competitive world of academia.

Meysel accepts the challenge and encounters many trials along the way including the House of GPA's, House of SAT (otherwise known as the College Board), House of Leadership, House of Extracurricular Activities, and House of Part-Time Employment.

Meysel emerges from her S/hero Quest triumphant as Valedictorian of her senior class. Ultimately, she vindicates her *abuelita* by accepting an invitation by the Lords of the Ivies to join them in a future battle.

This is a silly example, but it makes a clear point. Most students reading this book have been called to action. They will have encountered many challenges, road blocks, and obstacles along their pathway to higher education. And, they have triumphantly emerged as a S/hero, ready for the journey to college.

In fact, let me share an actual example of the S/hero journey. We'll call this student Lourdes. Lourdes balanced the risk of writing about a politically hot topic (see Chapter 11, Mistakes 6 & 8) and being able to share her authentic voice. She felt the S/hero Journey was central to her identity, and could not imagine writing a more meaningful response to Prompt No. 1 of the 2014/2015 Common Application:

Facing *La Bestia*

"The river, the Rio Suchiate, forms the border. Behind him is Guatemala. Ahead is Mexico, with its southernmost state of Chiapas. "Ahora nos enfrentamos a la bestia," migrants say when they enter Chiapas. 'Now we face the beast.'"

When I read this quote by author Sonia Nazario, I stopped breathing. The room became small and I could no longer hear my teacher. I am sitting in my AP English Literature & Composition class, but I am not reading Sonia Nazario's words. These are my words, my thoughts. This is my recount of facing La Bestia. Our teacher had assigned us "Enrique's Journey: The True Story of a Boy Determined to Reunite with His Mother. I thought it was a book about an adopted child or a boy caught in a child custody battle between his father and mother. It was neither — it was my story.

How do I know La Bestia? I met La Bestia in 2007. That summer, my brother and I stuffed our backpacks with water, food, one change of clothes, and one photograph of our parents. In our socks we placed a list of emergency contacts, telephone numbers, and $200 in cash. Sadly, we said goodbye to our relatives in San Pedro Sula, and fought the urge to remain with them in Honduras. We were on our way as unaccompanied children, to be reunited with our parents in Milkwaukee, Wisconsin. We had not seen our parents since 1997.

The road from San Pedro Sula to Wisconsin was nightmarish. In addition to facing La Bestia, my brother and I encountered many difficult obstacles along our path including dessert heat, starvation, and the constant fear of being victimized by ruthless individuals. Our strategy was to be invisible — keep quiet, and blend in.

Truthfully, throughout the entire journey I was terrified. However, my fear was overcome by my courage to see my parents. I had not seen my parents since I was three months old. I only knew their faces from a photograph.

My fear was also overcome by my dream to earn a college degree. I desperately wanted an education because I loved to learn. In San Pedro Sula, we did not *have a library or a Barnes & Noble. My only access to reading and learning was through a makeshift "Internet Café" terminal. From 2002 until the day I left San Pedro Sula in 2007, I read more than 100 books online and taught myself math and basic English. Years later, I learned the Internet Café was a front for a drug trafficker.*

The road from San Pedro Sula to Chiapas to Wisconsin was grueling. Looking back, I'm still unsure how I was able to survive. Perhaps it was my drive to succeed? Or, perhaps I was guided by a higher power. Today I'm both overwhelmed and grateful that I earned Valedictorian status at my high school, developed close friendships, and mastered the English language. Looking back at my journey from Honduras to Wisconsin reminds me of La Bestia. I know I will face many more beasts as I begin undergraduate studies and pursue a rigorous engineering pathway. However, the skills and characteristics I developed so far will enable me to conquer the many beasts I may encounter along my future academic journey.

While your S/hero's Journey or Quest may not be as prolific as Lourdes', you can see that the basic structure allows you to easily and effectively capture how you experienced and overcame the challenges along your life's journey.

How would this work for you? Let's break it down. Start with the "Call to Action." Your call to action could be from anyone — a mentor, teacher, coach, or relative. Or, it could have been *your own* call to action, through a personal epiphany, revelation, or spiritual experience.

Perhaps this person or experience prompted you to take some type of action. The action might be to challenge yourself in a particular subject matter, to run for a leadership position, to learn a second or third language, or to try out for the cross country team.

Next, you will describe how you embarked on this journey and encountered trials and tribulations. Using the examples above, the journey might be two years of AP Calculus, months of practicing your speech for class president, joining a language club, or spring training for cross country. Your job is to write about the challenges and triumphs you experienced along your journey.

Finally, you will redeem yourself and emerge triumphantly, as a S/hero! You will want to list redeeming qualities that emerged as a result of your trials and tribulations. For example, stamina to withstand the rigor of calculus, confidence to speak in public, patience to learn multiple languages, or physical and mental strength to endure long-distance training.

But, let's not forget this is a college essay! In your closing paragraphs you will want to accomplish two things. First, you'll want to incorporate how these qualities are related to your ability to succeed at a competitive university.

Second, the authentic S/hero's quest is a selfless act. Therefore, you'll want to frame your redeeming qualities in the larger context of a gift or treasure to share with humanity — whether within your immediate community or the extended community of academia. Your challenge is to articulate how your newfound gifts can be shared with the world, to make it a better place.

Tip!

The S/hero's Journey may not work with all essay prompts. For example, it may be suitable for the Common Application prompts 1, 3, and 5, but not so much in response to prompts 2 and 4.

Recap

The S/hero's Journey is a highly effective
Personal Statement strategy.
It is also referred to as the Hero's Quest or the Hero's Journey.

This storytelling structure has been used in literary works
across millennia and across nearly all cultures.

It is a five-step process:
Individual identified as being "special."
Receives a call to action.
With supernatural assistance, embarks on a journey.
Encounters trials and tribulations, and redeems her/himself.
Emerges as a S/hero.

Part Four

Blunders to Avoid

11

Top 10 Mistakes Students Make

So far, you've learned what you *should* include in your Personal Statement. In this chapter, you will learn how to avoid some huge blunders. These blunders are not simply recommendations.

They are big, fat, neon red road blocks that scream: *Alto! Don't go down that road!*

Before we delve into the 10 mistakes, let me share a few general rules. *Por favor*, do not talk about your pets. Seriously, admissions folks don't want to read about your amazing parrot *"Panchito"*, or "Maxwell," the cutest beagle ever. Ditto for discussing, "50 reasons why I have the greatest mom in the world!"

Lastly, don't be defiant or stubborn and dismiss or reject the concept of the traditional Personal Statement format. Students mistakenly believe their clever, creative, or humorously unique, "non-essay" will set them apart from other candidates. Don't go there. It's too risky. Very rarely does the rogue essay writer craft an innovative, non-conforming style or format that impresses the admissions readers.

Now, on to the "Top 10" mistakes:

Application and Essay Inconsistency
Separate Essay for Extenuating Circumstances
Blissful Naïveté
The "Ick" Factor
It's About Them, Not You
Too Much Information (TMI)
Inappropriate Topic
Political Hot Buttons
Just be Yourself . . . Not!
Colloquialisms, Euphemisms, and Slang

Mistake No. 1
Application and Essay Inconsistency

In the rush of assembling your application and essay, you may neglect to review whether your overall application "flows." An application and essay are inconsistent when any of the following occurs:

1. Your essay refers to cultural authenticity, but you lack consistency in the demographic and activities section on your application;
2. Your essay indicates a particular academic or service profile, but the profile within your application is significantly dissimilar;
3. Your course listings on your application indicate enrollment in ESL or ELL curriculum, yet your essay is suspiciously polished, reflecting an advanced native, or college level writer;
4. Your essay boasts extraordinary accomplishments, yet the extracurricular section of your application does not reflect these accomplishments.

Bottom line? Review your application contents against the content of your Personal Statement. Make sure the Statement compliments your overall profile and is consistent with the contents of your application.

Mistake No. 2
Separate Essay for Extenuating Circumstances

Extenuating circumstances in this context refers to barriers that prohibited the student from performing to the best of his or her abilities.

Many students have extenuating circumstances that critically impact their academic profile and standing. For example, perhaps there were multiple long-distance moves that required the student to transfer to six different high schools. Or, what if the student had a debilitating illness that impacted two years' worth of studies? Students sometimes make the mistake of utilizing their Personal Statement to provide background and detail to explain these circumstances.

The Personal Statement is not the place to defend yourself or explain discrepancies in your record. Instead, the colleges provide a perfect avenue for students to explain an academic deficiency. At the end of the application, there is typically a section that reads, *"You may use the Additional Information area in the Writing section to share relevant information about yourself that is not captured elsewhere in the application."*

Use this supplemental section to explain circumstances in a logical and quantifiable manner. Cause-and-effect is key. What caused the obstacle and what was the effect? Be realistic about what constitutes extenuating circumstances. Getting a B- on an AP Chemistry exam is not an extenuating circumstance.

However, there is an exception to Mistake No. 2. The exception is for students who decide to incorporate extenuating circumstances into their essay as a strategy to discuss key characteristics. This may be an appropriate strategy if the spotlight is *not* on the circumstances but on the skills learned or characteristics developed as a result of the circumstances.

Mistake No. 3
Blissful Naïveté

Naïveté is defined as, "lack of experience, wisdom, or judgment." Therefore, "Blissful Naïveté" is when a student doesn't realize s/he lacks this experience, wisdom, or judgment.

When children are young, they enjoy a blissful naïveté where anyone can aspire to be an astronaut, brain surgeon, or President of the United States. We encourage this mindset because we want them to set high standards and develop a healthy self-esteem. However, as they mature and begin to develop critical thinking skills, they also begin to temper lofty aspirations with reality and common sense.

For example, if a student receives C's and D's in math and biology, and scored a "2" on the Biology and Chemistry AP exams, this student may realize a career in veterinary medicine may not be aligned with his/her academic profile.

My point is that maturity and pragmatism should be apparent within a college essay. Otherwise, the goals within the essay may come across as naïve, pretentious, frivolous, and worse yet, unachievable. Remember, we want the admissions staff to "buy into" our Personal Statement. Our goal is for the reader to say, "Yeah, this kid is on the right track. I'm convinced she will reach her goals; and she will be a great addition to our incoming freshman class."

Naïveté may also be demonstrated by oversimplifying a concept within your essay. This holds especially true when the topic or concept is related to the major you will pursue as an undergraduate.

A few years ago, one of my students emailed me a draft essay regarding a true account of a hate crime. The essay focused on a victim (a recent Mexican immigrant) who was pushed into an irrigation ditch by self-proclaimed white supremacists and left to die. In describing the reason for this disturbing racist act, the writer simplified the perpetrators actions through a quote as a way to explain the consequence: "*Some people are good and some people are bad.*" Unfortunately, this explanation does not adequately or appropriately work within this context. It may seem simplistic, apathetic, and inappropriate.

My point? Complex topics like racism and hate crimes deserve thoughtful, careful analysis. Be cautious when trying to tackle a complex political or psychological issue. Otherwise, you risk sounding simplistic or naïve. Remember, we want you to convey you have the intellectual depth to be successful within a rigorous college program.

Another example of blissful naïveté is to project goals that appear excessively impractical. For example, one of my students declared in his essay that his academic goal was to pursue a double major. While it is perfectly fine to set aggressive goals, the combination of the two majors were highly impractical: Engineering and Political Science. Majoring in engineering is highly challenging. It is rigorous, competitive, and time-intensive. Add to this an entirely new set of prerequisites for a political science program, and these combined goals do not seem realistically feasible.

The bottom line: Colleges want their students to be successful. The admissions team will consider a student's past performance and academic profile to determine whether s/he is equipped to accomplish their stated future academic goals.

> **Tips!**
> Maturity, common sense, and pragmatism should not be misinterpreted as cynicism or lack of confidence. If you have the potential, personal disposition, and the academic profile consistent with your aspirations, then you should articulate this credibility within your essay.

Balance confidence and diligence by providing evidence that supports your endeavors. For example, if you state your goal is to become a national, syndicated journalist, then include examples of how you wrote for the school newspaper, won an essay writing competition, scored a perfect "5" on your AP English Exam, and achieved A's in AP English.

Mistake No. 4
The "Ick" Factor

This refers to the "icky" feeling we get when we read an essay with details that makes our skin crawl. This occurs when students try to build intensity and interest in their essay by being melodramatic.

The problem is the melodramatic essay ends up sounding cliché and forced. Instead of eliciting a positive reaction in your reader, one of two things happen. Either your reader will get grossed out and feel "icky," or they will roll their eyes. They will roll their eyes because it will be obvious the writer is pandering to elicit a strong emotion. Here is an example of an icky introductory paragraph:

My autoimmune disease symptoms begin with a fever and profuse sweating. Then, red, itchy, burning skin lesions appear on my face and arms. When the lesions burst, they ulcerate and form open sores. The sores ooze pus that smells like rotten eggs and forms a brownish crust . . .

Ick. This is just gross. I'm not trying to make fun of anyone with a skin disease. However, an essay is not the place to discuss rupturing open sores. There is a difference between naming a disease, in technical terms, and articulating how the student overcame this obstacle.

Here is another example:

His eyes rolled to the back of his head. Spit foam spilled out of the side of his mouth, and I heard him moaning in agony. Finally, he fell to the floor and hit his head on the wall. He then began convulsing violently. Shortly thereafter, he urinated on himself, his body stiffened, and he fell into a deep sleep.

These disturbing details describe the writer's account of her father's epileptic seizures. We feel saddened by this account, but it does not add to what we know about the writer. And, it borders on pandering for sympathy. In addition, the reader may find the account somewhat offensive and disrespectful — not appreciating the student's sharing of personal details concerning her father's suffering.

Unfortunately, the reader will likely remain fixated on the image of the father on the floor with foam oozing from his mouth. To turn this essay around, the writer should concisely (and in technical terms) state that she witnessed her father's trauma with epilepsy, and then describe what she gained from the experience. The focus should be on the student; not on the father.

Bottom line: When a student tries to gratuitously build intensity and interest by using melodramatic details, the reader will very likely feel "icky." Worse yet, the reader's takeaway will be their visceral reaction to the details, and not focused on the scholar. This is not the reaction we want.

Mistake No. 5
It's About Them, Not You

Sometimes the prompt asks you to identify a person who has impacted you in some significant way. It's an honorable question, for sure. But, the way in which students typically respond will yield what I call a "homage" essay. This means the student spends the entire essay talking about the influencer, and forgets to talk about him/herself!

For example, if I spend 650 words describing the awesomeness of my 11th grade AP history teacher, how will my homage inform the admissions reader about *me*?

The key to responding to this type of prompt is to follow this three-step strategy:

In the first paragraph, introduce the individual. For example, "The person who has greatly influenced my decision to pursue higher education was my cross country coach, Mr. Olivares."

In the second paragraph, tell the reader *how* the individual impacted *you*. For example,

> *Coach Olivares was instrumental in encouraging me to go to college. He took our team to visit local universities, brought in guest speakers, and assisted us with our financial aid forms. Through Coach Olivares' encouragement, I realized college was a reality. From this encouragement, I was able to accomplish . . .*

In the last paragraphs, describe the outcomes. For example,

> *Having developed a new perspective concerning four-year universities, I am now in a position to apply to colleges closely aligned with my academic profile and major.*

Tip!
Make sure the outcome you describe in step three is related to your ambition and preparedness as a potential undergraduate student.

Mistake No. 6
Too Much Information (TMI)

High school students tend to be very honest. Coupled with their honesty, they often treat their Personal Statement as a *personal* journal entry. Yikes. Let me show you a few examples:

"Being bullied as a child, thoughts of suicide ran through my mind . . ."

"My alcoholic father would stumble into my bedroom late at night . . ."

"Growing up as an undocumented student . . ."

Too much information disclosed in an essay can make the reader uncomfortable. Furthermore, if you are an undocumented student, disclosing your status may place you in a vulnerable position.

However, **I'm not saying** you shouldn't write about such experiences. If you feel compelled to discuss a sensitive topic because it is central to your identity, there are strategies.

For example, recall Lourdes' compelling essay entitled, "Facing *La Bestia*" describing her journey as a ten-year old undocumented student traveling from Honduras to the United States to be reunited with her parents. On the flip side, to view an inappropriate example of a "TMI" essay see Chapter 12 *"Essays Gone Wrong*!

Mistake No. 7
Inappropriate Topic

There is an overlap between including "Too Much Information" (TMI) in your essay and writing about an inappropriate topic. These two red-flag issues tend to go hand-in-hand, but not always.

Inappropriate topics generally include personal topics such as your sex life, drug addiction, illegal activities, eating disorders, incest, mental illness, academic dishonesty, or a learning disability, to name a few. Here are three examples of the inappropriate topics of an illegal activity, academic cheating, and a learning disability:

Example 1: *I wondered whether we would ever get caught. Me and my three friends have been sneaking into the Plaza de Oro movie theater since we were ten years old. Brandon would let us in through the Fire Exit door. Or, Jordan would cause a commotion and we'd casually walk right past the ticket-taker. The best trick: theater hopping! Either way, we were getting to watch movies for free.*

Example 2: *I struggle with cheating. Since the fourth grade, I have relied on cheating to complete my homework and in-class projects. It seems far easier and effortless to borrow a classmate's answer or pilfer a few nuggets of wisdom from an open answer sheet on my teacher's desk. I'm not proud of my cheating, but I feel the effort to complete my own work is not worth it.*

Example 3: *I am constantly fidgeting and squirming in my seat. My classmates barely tolerate my non-stop talking. If I didn't have a pencil and pencil sharpener on my desk, my hands would frantically grab and play with anything in sight. The worst part about my diagnosed Attention Deficit Hyperactivity Disorder, is that I have great difficulty completing tasks and activities. This disorder has significantly impacted my ability to complete assignments, class projects, and maintain appropriate grades.*

Why does Quetzal Mama advise you *not* to attempt tackling these inappropriate and sensitive topics? Aside from the obvious, admissions staff are also viewing your Personal Statement from another angle.

In addition to evaluating your application and essay to determine whether you can handle the academic work, colleges *also* evaluate the soft skills we discussed in the beginning of this book. They want to know whether or not you will thrive and be a contributing member at their campus. Their goal is similar to yours — they want you to be successful. Therefore, they are sensitive to identifying issues, stressors, psychological dispositions, learning disabilities, or anything else that may indicate a difficult college experience.

Exemption Disclaimer

If the topic is central to your identity, has significantly influenced the way you see the world, and has resulted in a positive outcome, then you might have an exception to my rule.

Or, if you have a learning disability and are specifically applying to colleges with strong learning disability programs, then it would be appropriate to discuss such a topic within your Personal Statement.

Or, if you are gifted writer and/or have conducted significant research on a very personal topic, you may be able to respond in a reflective and analytical manner. However, these writers tend to be the exceptional, rather than the typical, high school student. A typical student may end up offending their reader, or worse yet, the reader determines the writer does not have the maturity or intellectual depth to discuss the topic.

Bottom line: You have an abundance of topics you may consider for your Personal Statement. Why take the risk of writing about an inappropriate topic? Instead, spend time brainstorming ideas that will positively enhance your profile.

Mistake No. 8
Political Hot Buttons

There is a fine line between the persuasive writer who eloquently and thoughtfully articulates a political point with sensitivity and dignity, and the writer who alienates the reader through a closed-minded, self-righteous, argumentative style. This fine line occurs when a student decides to write about a touchy topic.

There are many touchy topics that — unless you are a skillful, politically savvy writer, you should avoid. Some of these topics include gay rights, immigration reform, abortion, the "war on terror," gun control, affirmative action, capital punishment, etc. However, there are students exempt from this rule. These are students who are involved, on the front lines, as social justice advocates. They have been involved in a particular cause or political movement and it would benefit them to discuss their involvement within their essay.

A great example is the student who has led a grass roots movement within their community regarding immigration rights. Perhaps the student holds a leadership position in a group such as Parents, Friends and Family of Lesbians and Gays (PFLAG). Again, the key is to write about the topic with sensitivity, dignity, and authenticity. To view a stellar example of a student who "nailed" a highly political topic (political asylum for a transgender student), see Amber Escobar's essay in Part Six.

Mistake No. 9
Just be Yourself . . . Not!

Visit any college admissions website and you will find that many colleges provide the following advice for writing the Personal Statement: *Just be yourself.*

Yeah. Sounds simple and effective. The *"be yourself"* concept seems honest, practical, and intuitive, yes? It is. As long as "yourself" is an ideal package that renders the coveted declaration: "Welcome to the Class of 2018!"

Recently, Pittsburgh high school student Suzy Lee Weiss wrote an article on this very topic published in the Wall Street Journal. The title of this piece: "To (All) the Colleges that Rejected Me," with the subtitle, "If Only I had a Tiger Mom or Started a Fake Charity." This Op-Ed piece was circulated around the world and landed Ms. Weiss with television interviews on Good Morning America and the Today Show, as well as acceptance to University of Michigan.

> *"Colleges tell you, 'Just be yourself.' That is great advice, as long as yourself has nine extracurriculars, six leadership positions, three varsity sports, killer SAT scores and two moms. Then by all means, be yourself!"*

The truth in her piece is that while colleges indeed wish to hear your authentic voice, there are simply some ways to enhance or weaken your profile. What colleges really want is for you to show them your true *"self"* through your academics, extracurricular activities, race/ethnicity, culture, service, or anything that shaped your character and how you perceive the world around you.

I'm not suggesting you embellish your essay to pander to the admissions reader. I am saying, just show your *best* self. This means to highlight those things that will look great on your application, and to avoid those things that do not. It also means to balance your fallibility carefully, but not to the point you downgrade your profile.

Here is an example. Think of online personal ads. Potential male suitors will show their *best* self by saying they are hard-working, financially responsible, and romantic. This may yield them better results. However, if they were to follow the "*be yourself*" guideline, and were truly honest and authentic, their ad might read something like this:

"I expect you to take care of all of the household chores because I am far too busy in my important job. And, my mother does not think any woman is good enough for me."

A profile statement like this would be disastrous. The online romancer should have enough sense to avoid damaging "truths" like this, and include positive elements that are more appealing.

Ditto for your essay. Avoid "*be yourself*" comments such as, "I may not be at the top of my class, but I try really hard." Or, "Most people have told me I won't amount to anything, but I will just try harder." Or, "I try to keep my clinical depression under control."

Why deflate your profile by adding negative (yet truthful) information? Be honest and *"be yourself,"* but not to the point where your honesty and authenticity yields an inferior profile.

Mistake No. 10
Colloquialisms, Euphemisms, and Slang

I was like, oh no you didn't!
For reals? Like I'm supposed to believe that?
Girl, that's cray cray!

Trust me on this last mistake — don't go there. Many students mistakenly write their essay in the same manner in which they speak with their peers. The vernacular of high school students is not suitable language for a college essay.

Colloquialisms are informal terms or phrases that are typically used within a particular region or organization. Don't make the mistake of using words or phrases that may only be understood by students of a particular age. For example, incorporating digital (text) lingo into an essay is too informal (and conveys immaturity) for a college essay.

Euphemisms are substitutions for the literal word or a blunt way of saying something. For example, stay away from silly euphemisms such as, "He kicked the bucket" or "He bit the dust," when you should say, "He is deceased," or "He died." Likewise, don't say "He blew chunks" if you intend to say he "vomited."

Slang can be described as informal words or phrases that may be inappropriate, lewd, or vulgar. For example, "junk in the trunk." The exception to using slang in a Personal Statement is to include a slang term *intentionally* by using quotation marks to denote the improper usage. The quotation marks around the term indicate you are denoting irony or sarcasm within your text through *irony punctuation*. For example, "His professor accused him of using the 'race card' to accentuate his point." However, be cautious in using irony punctuation appropriately and effectively. Novice writers run the risk of improperly using this literary tool. Consequently, they may unintentionally convey arrogance, smugness, or immaturity.

Bottom line: You want your essay to sound authentic so that your voice comes through. Therefore, don't use language that sounds phony or contrived. Your goal is to tell your story by delicately balancing your authentic, personal, friendly voice *and* respecting the formality of the college essay.

12

Essays Gone Wrong!

*O*n this chapter, I will highlight four ill-advised and misguided essay themes. After describing how these essay themes have "gone wrong," I will provide an example of how to turn the essay around — to "Nail it!"

The Abstract, Philosophical, Cryptic Essay

Who are we? We find that we live on an insignificant planet of a humdrum star lost in a galaxy tucked away in some forgotten corner of a universe in which there are far more galaxies than people. —Carl Sagan

Rarely can a high school student pull off the enormous task of tackling Personal Statements that ponder life's mysteries and complexities. More often than not, students who attempt to conquer philosophical questions may come across as impersonal and aloof. Their essay may touch gloomy or dark topics, gothic themes, or anything that leaves the reader feeling fatalistic, dark, depressed, gothic, desolate, or cryptic. Another abstract pitfall is to write in a "Stream of Consciousness." See *Glossary* for definition.

What does abstract, philosophical, or cryptic writing look like? Here is an example from a student I'll call Diego. Diego is truly brilliant and gifted. His SAT scores and AP exams were off the charts. In speaking with him, it was clear he was far more introspective and mature compared to his peers. However, his attempt to articulate his view of the world came across as "out there.":

> *How easily a multitude of ink blotches on a bunch of dead tree could transport me to a world beyond my own, one so far away, with its fantastical creations of heroism and villainy alike, but yet so close, reflecting on my very own life.*

In a gentle way, I steered Diego away from strolling down this philosophical pathway. I reminded Diego that the Personal Statement is not an abstract space where we theorize or ponder. Instead, we strategized how we could showcase his cultural authenticity and depth of intellect in his essay.

We chose to present the Mayan concept of Dualism to explain his interesting perspective of the world and himself. In this way, he was able to highlight cultural authenticity, passion for the engineering discipline (referring to the Mayan's contributions in mathematics), and his intellectual prowess.

Let's read how Diego responded to the Common Application Prompt No. 4: "Describe a place or environment where you are perfectly content."

> *In Western culture, we tend to view contentedness as being synonymous with happiness. We avoid states of being that are counter to our ideal of happiness such as negativism, adversity, anger, or sorrow. However, I was raised in Central America practicing the Mayan principle of Dualism. In my world, contentedness is achieved by simultaneously experiencing and embracing conflicting states of being. My cultural upbringing taught me to appreciate both positive and negative*

aspects of human existence including love and hate, fear and confidence, be-
nevolence and malevolence, vanity and humility. Through this understanding, I
am able to experience "ahuia" — the Nahuatl term for contentedness.

The "Whiny, Woe is Me" Essay

Read my heart wrenching story. I am a victim.
Feel sorry for me. I need pity.
Will you admit me now?

The Latino students I coach have many, many obstacles. Some of my students live in tin shacks — exposed to extreme weather, pesticides, and other dangerous chemicals. Others work full time, on weekends and summers, in scorching 100 degree plus heat, packing fruit and vegetable crates for a measly daily wage. When these students craft their essays, I encourage them to include carefully selected details to illustrate their unique life experiences, but to avoid negative language that could potentially characterize them as a "victim."

While it is tempting for some students to include heart-wrenching details, in hopes it may make the admissions reader feel guilty and sympathetic, I strongly advise against this. Why? The admissions reader wants to feel inspired, not guilty. Some key identifiers of a victim-themed essay include the following:

1. The essay conveys no personal responsibility for life's events or circumstances;
2. The essay conveys a conspiracy mindset — everyone and everything is against this student;

3. The essay conveys a sense of concession and defeat, rather than a spirit of will and triumph; and

4. Worse yet, the essay seems to be the student's *entire* life story, not just a backdrop that enhances their overall profile.

This type of essay is a "Doom and Gloom" essay in that it focuses on negative topics, has a somber tone, and leaves the reader feeling depressed and uninspired. This is the exact opposite effect you are seeking! You want your reader to feel inspired and positively charged. What does a "victim" essay look like? Here is an example written by Tonantzin:

> *My family represents the stereotype that exists for many Mexicans, that we are landscapers, janitors, or maids. My father has worked his entire life as a janitor, cleaning disgusting filth and bringing home a measly paycheck. My mother has not done better. She cleans the homes of people who treat her like a second class citizen. Sometimes I think I should give up, and just forego my dreams of going to college.*

You can see that Tonantzin is conveying a sense of defeat and concession, versus a sense of triumph and will. We don't hear Tonantzin's scholarly voice. Instead, she articulates pessimism, resentment, and futility. How could Tonantzin turn this around to convey optimism, will, and *ganas*? Here is a revised version of this same paragraph:

> *At a young age, I became aware of a common stereotype that exists about Mexican-Americans. The stereotype is that our position in society is limited to menial and labor-intensive occupations such as janitors, maids, and landscapers. However, at a young age I also became determined to defy that stereotype*

and to pursue a career as a software engineer. Rather than dwelling on what others may perceive of me, I chose to follow my own dream and to create my own path.

Referring to the same obstacles and concepts in the previous paragraph, Tonantzin changes the tone (negative to positive) by claiming her destiny. She acknowledges obstacles, but describes how she refuses to allow the obstacles to dictate her future. Her life story is not about her obstacles, but rather how she has overcome them (positive qualities). She nailed it!

The Overly Confident, "It's All About Me!" Essay

I am so wonderful. I serve underlings and the peasantry. I help impoverished, less fortunate souls. I was class president and hold the highest GPA in my entire school. Plus, I'm super good looking.

In my practice, it is extremely rare I come across an essay that sounds overly confident, cocky, or arrogant and pretentious. Most of the students I coach *downplay* their extraordinary accomplishments. Worse yet, many of these gifted students neglect to mention their unique and compelling attributes. Why don't they?

In Latino culture, we are taught it is not proper to brag, boast, or bring attention to ourselves. We are taught to be humble, and let our accomplishments speak for themselves. While this is honorable and admirable, it is a liability when it comes to the Personal Statement. However, balancing the honorable quality of being humble, with assertively demonstrating core strengths, can be a tricky tight rope walk.

What does an overly confident essay look like? These types of essays exude arrogance and self-righteousness, and they read like a resume. They sound competitive and braggadocios. Bottom line: They are boring and obnoxious. Below is an example illustrating this point:

> *In my sophomore year I was elected Vice President of the Interact Club. I am the only person in my class, and in the history of my school, to have been selected as Vice President as a sophomore. I also serve as President of the Associated Student Body, and was elected due to my exceptional intellect and my extraordinarily charismatic personality.*

How do you know if your Personal Statement cleverly weaves accomplishments or is just plain bragging? I'll tell you! Here are the red flags that will alert you that your Personal Statement is full of hot air:

- Overuse of "I" statements. This means most of your paragraphs begin with "I." For example, "I am the best student in my class," or "I was elected Class President," or "I was chosen to serve on the . . ."

- The statement reads like a resume. Typically, these statements read in chronological order, listing all of the accomplishments of the student. For example, "In my freshman year, I did x, y, and z." "In my sophomore year, I did x, y, and z." You get the point.

- The tone is condescending. The student doesn't come out and say, "I am better than everyone else," but may as well have. There is a fine balance between articulating empathy and sounding like a benevolent glory seeker.

Then tell me, Quetzal Mama, how can I include my accomplishments without bragging?

The "Oh, incidentally" Strategy — There is a clever way to interweave accomplishments into a Personal Statement without sounding conceited or boring. I call it the "Oh, incidentally" strategy. It works like this. In writing about a topic or event you, "incidentally," throw in a personal fact or accomplishment. Here is an example from a student we will call, "Patricia."

> *Although innovative scientific research programs are non-existent in my hometown of Coachella, California, I knew that my independent nanotechnology research focused in Atom Transfer Radical Polymerization would prepare me to compete with scholars in the Siemens Competition in Math, Science & Technology.*

Do you see how in this one sentence, Patricia is able to showcase her accomplishments without bragging or sounding arrogant? Without actually saying it, she cleverly wove into her essay:

· I am very bright.

· I am a female, competing in a discipline dominated by males.

· I can do extraordinary research, even without adequate preparation.

- I did not have the resources of other students, yet I am able to compete at their level.

- I competed in a national science competition.

Patricia veered away from saying, "I am so great and extraordinary." However, the reader can infer this fact through her statements. Cleverly, important facts were *incidentally* thrown into her statement. By adding details such as the type of research conducted and the name of the competition, she adds interest, qualifies her academic profile, and allows the reader to make a positive judgment. The bottom line: Patricia rocks, and she "nailed it!"

The TMI, Journal Entry Essay

Loaded with confidential issues, such as mental health, sex life, substance abuse, addiction, rape, incest, abortion, immigration status, or any topic that is no one's business!

TMI means "Too Much Information." It is considered inappropriate to discuss any confidential topic (such as those above) in your Personal Statement. The content of your essay should represent your "essence" or unique qualities. Unless you believe the issue defines you and you can *sensitively and appropriately* discuss how it helped shape your academic profile, then you should not include it in your essay. It is very challenging to address a confidential topic in an appropriate way — without risking that your reader will feel awkward, embarrassed, alienated, or disturbed.

Sometimes, a student will want to address a confidential topic in his/her statement because the student believes it shaped his/her academic profile and/or career aspirations. Last year, a student (we'll call her "Elisa") asked me to help her edit her Personal Statement. Her statement contained confidential information about being a victim of physical abuse. She provided excessive details about the type of abuse she suffered, the methods her abuser employed, and the frequency of the abuse.

The details were far too titillating. Consequently, her essay had a very negative tone and did not say much about her. The reader was naturally focused on the abuser and not the student.

In this case, it was clear Elisa felt this life experience shaped who she had become: a survivor. We decided this was an exception to the "TMI" rule and worked sensitively and appropriately to include this topic in her essay.

Elisa began her essay with a quote by Dr. Martin Luther King, Jr.: *"Violence is the last refuge of the incompetent."* While Elisa discussed being a victim of domestic violence, she focused instead on how as a survivor, she views the world differently. She discussed how her experience, ironically, empowered her. She wrote about how the result of her experience led her to pursue undergraduate and graduate level studies in order to become a champion against domestic abuse. Read Elisa's conclusion below, and see how she turned a negative into a positive:

> *As a senior in high school, I can now look back and view my family environment in a clearer and objective manner. I now find comfort and inspiration from*

Dr. King's words because I have learned violent persons are not powerful — they are weak and incompetent. It is this conviction that has compelled me to use my academic talents toward helping others survive domestic violence. This unique perspective is the driving force that inspires me to pursue undergraduate studies that will broaden my knowledge and eventually prepare me for law school. As an attorney, I believe my skills and talents can be utilized in ways to serve those without a voice.

As mentioned above, this essay is an exception to the "TMI" rule. Generally, I would strongly advise against disclosing sensitive information in your statement. However, if you are considering writing about a sensitive topic in your Personal Statement, first ask yourself these questions:

1. Does my essay convey my "essence"; my unique and positive qualities?
2. Does my essay focus too much on the topic, situation, or conflict, instead of me?
3. Does my essay disclose information that will make the reader feel uncomfortable, awkward, or embarrassed?

Finally, if you do decide that you wish to talk about a sensitive topic in your Personal Statement, make sure that you get a second opinion from your parents or high school guidance counselor.

Part Five

But Wait, There's More!

13

Supplemental Essays

Just when you thought you nailed the Personal Statement, you learn many colleges also require a Supplemental Essay! A Supplemental Essay is a question or set of questions, relatively short in length, that focus on a very narrow topic. Students overlook the importance of these essays and whiz through them quickly and carelessly.

Before we discuss Supplemental Essay writing strategies, you may be wondering why you are required to write these additional essays in the first place? Simply put, the supplemental essays accomplish two goals for the admissions reader.

First, it gives the reader additional information regarding your interests and academic plans, specific to their university. It tells the reader whether you are a good fit for them; and whether they are a good fit for you.

Second, it helps the admissions team project their "yield." The yield is the number of students who *accept* their offer of admission, in comparison to the total number of students who were offered admission. The yield, therefore, is a percentage. As you can imagine, competitive universities want to keep their yield (or acceptance percentage) high. Remember, status is very much a part of this high stakes game. If only 50 percent of students accept an offer of admission, it does not bode well for the university's image or status.

The thinking goes like this: If you can name their specific programs, resources, and idiosyncrasies, chances are you *really want* to attend the university. Therefore, the content within the supplemental essay will likely demonstrate whether or not you've done your homework. In this case, doing the "homework" equates to your genuine interest level. For admission folks, interest = yield.

Students commonly fumble in this area by responding to the supplemental essay prompt(s) in vague ways. For example, when asked why the student is applying to the college campus, students commonly refer to the name and prestige of the campus, recite the college mission statement, or discuss the beauty of the architecture. For example,

> *I'm applying to Yale because it is always in the top three rankings of the U.S. News & World Report. I also enjoy the gothic architecture and the beautifully landscaped grounds.*

An admissions officer will not view these as compelling reasons for your admission.

Instead, you should focus on *specific* details that convinced you to apply. For example, the research facilities or internship opportunities relevant to your major, renowned faculty, on-campus support groups, or rigor of curriculum within your chosen major. Each response should be carefully crafted to sound convincing for the greatest impact. For example,

> *Because of my interest in Neuroscience, courses such as, "How the Brain Works," "Neurobiology" (and lab), and "Brain Development and Plasticity" influenced my decision to apply to Yale. Aside from the curriculum, the research laboratories available within the neuroscience discipline were also influential. In addition to my studies, non-academic activities offered at Yale that are appealing to me include AISES, Yale Swing & Blues, Mathcounts Outreach, and Yale Minorities in Medicine Movement.*

For the "Why us?" supplemental question, the first portion of your essay should reflect the academic factors that shaped your decision. This means you should focus at least 50 percent of this supplemental essay on factors that relate to the major you have chosen. The remaining 50 percent may include other factors such as social, cultural, sports, or on-campus organizations.

In addition to the "why us" question, many selective universities want to know about your "intellectual curiosity."

Below is an example of an outstanding response to Stanford's supplement. See how Miguel exercises his intellectual "muscle" and demonstrates with ease how he would fit in perfectly with other intellectually curious students at Stanford. The Stanford prompt was as follows: "Stanford students are widely known to possess a sense of intellectual vitality. Tell us about an idea or an experience you have had that you find intellectually engaging."

An experience that has been important to my intellectual development was one of my first organic chemistry labs on nucleophilic substitution reactions. In this lab, I had one substrate with high steric hindrance and one with low steric hindrance. I introduced nucleophiles to each substrate in order to observe which produced the most product substance.

Though this was an unordinary experiment to conduct in a chemistry lab, this experience was exciting and fascinating to me because of the new concepts I learned. I became interested in the mechanisms that drive reactions in a particular direction—such as free energy and its influence towards making the most thermodynamically stable product, or the interactions between the highest occupied molecular orbital and lowest unoccupied molecular orbital (HOMO and LUMO) in order to form particular bonds as described by the molecular orbital theory.

Furthermore, I became captivated by scientists' abilities to synthesize, theoretically, any type of molecule through basic chemical and engineering principles.

Miguel did not "dumb down" his essay for fear that the admissions reader would not "get it." Instead, he felt confident describing his interest in chemistry in a highly technical way. Yes, he could have said simply, "I am interested in the field of chemistry." However, by providing specific details and referring to technical terms, the admissions reader will glean a lot more about this candidate's passion for chemistry (and intellectual curiosity).

Final Tip!

Now is not the time to be shy or convey doubts. This additional essay is your opportunity to provide "proof" as to why you should be admitted. This is the time to advocate for yourself and "seal the deal." Avoid wishy-washy, non-committal language. There are compelling reasons why you chose this campus: Tell them!

Recap

Do your "homework."

Provide compelling reasons why you wish to attend the college.

Provide *specific* details, not broad generalities.

Focus on academic factors first, followed by non-academic.

Academic factors should comprise at least 50 percent of your essay.

Advocate for yourself.

Sound convincing (no wishy-washy answers).

14

Requests for More Information

What if you get one of those, "We need more information" emails from a selective university? It happens. It's pretty rare, but it does happen. What are these letters? They are very rare inquiries from a university seeking additional information before they can render their admission decision.

A handful of my students have received these requests through the years. These requests ask you to provide an additional essay(s) in response to specific prompts. Don't panic! As I tell my students, "If they are asking you for more information, it means as of this moment you haven't been denied!" Seriously, if you received one, there are some basic strategies to follow. But first, let's look at some of the questions asked.

For example, UC Berkeley's recent questionnaire contained 13 questions, asking the student to respond to each question so they can ". . .*carefully review your responses as we make admission decisions.*"

UC Davis recently sent a questionnaire that read: *"As part of our comprehensive review, would you like us to consider the extreme hardship or difficult circumstances (medical, personal, judicial) that you have disclosed to us?"*

In any event, they are not asking you to submit another 650-word essay! In reality, they are exercising due diligence. This means they do not wish to overlook any factors that may unfairly preclude you from admission. They want to ensure they are following their admission protocols and allowing the student to explain any extenuating circumstances

What are they looking for? They are *not* looking for the student to regurgitate what he/she included in the application. If the information in the application was sufficient, the student would not be asked to elaborate or explain further.

They are trying to understand, in a logical and reasonable way, how a claimed disadvantage precluded or prohibited the student from performing at his/her ability or potential.

In this scenario, the student should be able to quantify and qualify the response. For example, if the student's GPA slipped for one academic year he/she should be able to articulate the specific obstacle(s) that impacted the performance. It should be logical, such as this:

> *During my junior year, my parents filed for divorce; and we moved to another school district. Moving to another school and dealing with the psychological impact of this change significantly affected my grades.*

This example can be proven because both the transcript (indicating a new school) and the cumulative academic record will illustrate a definite correlation between the event and the GPA dip.

In addition to responding to the email questionnaire, the student may be required to submit updated and official transcripts, new test scores, or an essay describing the reason(s) the student wishes to receive admission to their campus.

Regardless of the request, my recommendation is to follow these general guidelines:

1. Respond as soon as possible, prior to the designated deadline.
2. Follow the directions carefully and submit or respond to every item requested.
3. Conduct research regarding the types of information requested, and potential reasons why the student may have been targeted.
4. Seek help from an experienced admissions consultant or high school counselor.
5. Contact the requester directly for more information.

Recap
It is uncommon for a student to receive a
"We Need More Information" inquiry.
If you receive such an inquiry, don't panic!
Follow the five steps outlined in this chapter.

15

Bonus Chapter - Transfer Student Essays

Community college transfer students are some of the most disciplined, incredible students you will meet. I began working with transfer students before the California Dream Act passed in 2011. Prior to this time, my undocumented students were ineligible to receive state or federal financial aid, and tragically, were forced to rescind their admission offers. Today, my California students are eligible to receive state aid in California, but are still ineligible for federal aid and student loans.

However, a wonderful thing emerged from this tragedy. I was able to work with Latino superstars while learning and developing Personal Statement strategies for transfer from a community college to a four-year university. I wrote this bonus chapter to provide tips, strategies, and effective methods for students who intend to transfer to a competitive four-year university.

Before you jump into the time-intensive essay-writing process, it is important that you carefully select the university that fits your academic needs and is aligned with your academic profile. For example, in fall 2014, Stanford only admitted 33 students, while MIT only admitted 21. Conversely, UC Berkeley admitted 3,825 students (or 23 percent of applicants). Make sure to strategize to which campuses you will submit an application *before* you begin writing your Personal Statements.

The first thing you need to know as a potential transfer student is that there are different essays required from different universities. See Part I, *"Overview of the College Application Essay."* For example, some universities, such as the University of Chicago, require completion of both the traditional Common Application prompt (650 words) as well as three additional Supplemental Essays for transfer student applicants. (See strategies for Supplemental Essays in Chapter 13.)

The second thing you need to know is that nearly all universities provide a unique and specially designed prompt for transfer student applicants. While the prompts may be designed exclusively for transfer students, these prompts (questions) tend to vary from campus to campus.

The third thing you need to know is that regardless of the prompts, these universities demand key information from transfer applicants. They want to know why you are transferring and why you chose a particular major. For this reason, the prompts tend to be very explicit. They may even have a prompt designed specifically for your major! Here is an example of a prompt designed for engineering transfer students applying to Duke University:

> *As a transfer applicant, please discuss why you want to study* **engineering** *and why you would like to study at Duke (150 words).*

While many universities provide specific transfer prompts or prompts focused on a particular major, other universities may require multiple essays. Regardless of the number of prompts, just remember that the university is looking for demonstration that you will be able to handle a rigorous four-year university curriculum, and that you have the discipline and aptitude to thrive in the major you selected.

Let's look at the University of California's 2014 prompt for transfer students. Note there are two required prompts (for a total of 1,000 words): one prompt designed for transfer students, and one designed for all candidates (including transfer students). Students must answer both prompts. Below is the transfer student prompt:

> *What is your intended major? Discuss how your interest in the subject developed and describe any experience you have had in the field — such as volunteer work, internships and employment, participation in student organizations and activities — and what you have gained from your involvement.*

Wow, that's loaded with questions, right? The easiest way to approach the UC transfer prompt is to follow the steps outlined in Chapter 4, "*Los Huesos.*" Using *Los Huesos*, let's identify the questioned asked. I see four (4) questions here:

1. What's your major?
2. How did you become interested in this particular major?
3. What are your *related* experiences within this major?
4. What have you gained from these experiences?

Following *Los Huesos* format you will grab a piece of paper and write down the answers to identified questions in the *simplest* form possible. Don't try to be fancy, clever, or sophisticated. Just answer each question in a sentence. You will have four sentences.

Question No. 1: What's Your Major?

First, before you address the "What's your major" question, you'll need to do your homework. Unless you're only applying to one campus, be sure the major you specify in your essay is *broad* enough to cover different majors offered at multiple campuses, but *specific* enough to demonstrate your genuine interest.

For example, you might declare Chicana/o Studies at UC Davis but find that UC San Diego does not offer this major! At UC San Diego you may declare Ethnic Studies or Latin-American Studies as an undergraduate major. In this instance, you can simply say: "My intended major is Ethnic Studies with an emphasis in Chicano/Latino Studies." This way, you capture the umbrella concept of Ethnic Studies, but introduce your particular interest in Chicano/Latino Studies.

Question No. 2:
How did you become interested in this particular major?

When approaching the second question, "How did you become interested in this particular major," contemplate your response from an evolutionary perspective. In other words, how did this major develop and *grow* on you? Maybe you always knew you wanted to study political science or be an aeronautical engineer? If so, then tell them! Tell them *when* your interest was ignited, *how* it grew, and *why* it has compelled you to declare this major.

Here are a few introductory examples. Keep in mind, these are only the introductory paragraphs. To read a few of these essays in their entirety, see the end of this chapter.

Example 1

Recently, I saw the question posed: What does it mean to 'think sociologically' and how does this differ from other ways of seeing the world around us?" This question intrigued me and represents one of the reasons I have chosen sociology as my intended major. My interest in sociology developed when I took my first sociology course in college. I was fascinated by how societal behaviors, whether at the micro or macro level, reflect the world in which we live.

Example 2

After taking my first college sociology course, I became fascinated. Having been raised on the "poor side of town," I was always aware of the many factors that divide the wealthy from those in poverty. However, it wasn't until I learned various sociological theories — such as symbolic Interactionism, Functionalism, and Conflict Theory, that I was able to articulate how this division impacts our communities and our world. Through my studies, I have come to understand the mentality of social inequality and social oppression. I knew I was poor, but did not realize how and why this factor implicates my life in complex ways. Most importantly, I have come to value how my Latino culture has helped me gain a better understanding of the complexities of sociological constructs.

Example 3

My intended major is chemical engineering. My interest in engineering developed early. At a very young age, I contemplated ideas and concepts that most students my age did not. For example, while most people would consider my family's home very small (it was only 600 square feet), I instead focused on the fact that each sibling occupied 204 cubic meters. While my parents, migrant field workers, warned us that the pesticides outside of our home could make us sick, I instead focused on how a pentachloralphenol compound compared to a Thiocarbomate compound. Or, how Chlorpyrifos chemically inhibits the enzyme acetyl cholinesterase.

Question No. 3:
What are your *related* experiences within this major?

Answering this question is a lot easier than most students realize. To gather content for this question, just grab your resume. Look at the activities you have been involved in throughout your tenure at the community college. For example, if you worked part time as a teacher's assistant or lab tutor in statistics, and you wish to transfer as an Applied Math major, you'll want to discuss these experiences within your essay. Or, what if you are the Treasurer of the Linguistics Club at the community college, and you are applying as a Spanish major? Bingo — include it! Here is an example of what this looks like:

One of the first courses I enrolled in at San José City College was Introduction to Philosophy. After reading the syllabi and sitting in a few lectures, I found this major intriguing. However, after taking a related course, Introductory Logic, I was certain I was in the right major. Learning formal techniques of sentential logic (concepts of induction, deduction, validity, soundness, strength, and cogency), sparked my interest. It seemed as if my mind intuitively grasped symbolic logic, natural deduction, and the calculation of probabilities.

My gravitation toward all things "philosophical" led me to join our campus Philosophy, Arts and Sciences Alliance (P.A.S.A.). Within this new network, I met other students who shared my inquisitive nature concerning truth, ethics, religion, language, arts, and other philosophical ponderings. Wishing to pursue a leadership position within this organization, I was elected President in 2014. Throughout my Presidency, our team has brought guest speakers and authors, and we've watched films to engage in philosophical discussions.

After reviewing your resume, now look to your official transcript. I encourage my transfer students to cite the highlights of their academic career at the community college, *relative* to his/her intended major. For example, if Gabriela is applying to UCLA as a Sociology major, she will want to emphasize the most rigorous and interesting coursework related to her major. She might say something like this:

> *While at Modesto Junior College, my interest in sociology was ignited. While taking Gender in Contemporary Society, I delved into fascinating comparative analysis of gender roles in the US, as well as theories in Feminist Studies. Discovering these new concepts compelled me to expand my learning by taking Social Inequality in the US, where I learned emerging theories concerning marginalized societies. Culminating this knowledge led me to seek approval from my Dean to conduct specialized studies within my growing interest of feminist studies.*

Tip!
Simply listing your academic accomplishments is redundant. Make it meaningful by carefully selecting relevant highlights. See Chapter 3, "Avoid Regurgitating the Application."

Question No. 4: What have you gained from these experiences? (aka "Y Que?")

This question begs you to describe the outcome from your experiences. It is the "so what" question: "So what" that you enjoy math and were a math tutor. *Y que?* Tell them ¡*y que*! Did it empower you to create free math workshops for at-risk youth in your community? Did it compel you to create a student chapter of the Association for Women in Mathematics? Did the experiences lead to an internship at IBM, igniting your desire to pursue a Ph.D. in mathematics? You get the point.

The bottom line: They are trying to assess your genuine interest within the discipline you declared. Tell the admissions folks by providing quantifiable metrics, demonstrated interest, and concrete "proof"

> **Tip!**
> Use the "Magical Power of Three" strategy (see Chapter 5).
> Give them three things you gained from your experiences.

Key Strategies for Transfer Student Prompts

Respond to questions in the order asked. Make it easy on yourself! A solid strategy is to answer the prompts in the order in which they are asked. It's a logical process because the questions asked are consistent with the chronology of your decision to declare a particular major.

For example, in the first paragraph you will declare your major succinctly, followed by the reason(s) you selected this major. In the second paragraph you will discuss the related experiences (rigorous coursework, work experience, activities on campus, etc.). In the third paragraph you will answer the "so what" question. In the final paragraph you tie it all together by summarizing how the cumulative effect of these experiences will make you an undergraduate superstar!

Speak to Your Audience. More so than ever, when addressing the Transfer Student prompt you want to practice the strategy outlined in Chapter 7, *TIN CASA*. Specifically, the "S" in Speak to Your Audience. In this case, the audience will definitely be faculty members within the major you are applying. Speak their language! Show them how you fit within their world, and how comfortable you are speaking in terms and referencing concepts that will surely resonate within their academic community.

Recap
Most colleges have a unique prompt for transfer students.
Colleges want to know why you are transferring.
Colleges want to know why you declared your major.
Follow *Los Huesos* strategy to get started.
Pay attention to the "¡Y Que?" question.
Use the Magical Power of Three.
Speak to your audience.

Now, enjoy the following student essays from two superstars transferring from a Community College to a University of California Campus

HOW MY INTEREST IN ENGINEERING DEVELOPED
Rodrigo Tellez
(UC Berkeley)

My intended major is chemical engineering. My interest in engineering developed early. At a very young age, I contemplated ideas and concepts that most

students my age did not. For example, while most people would consider my family's home very small (it was only 600 square feet), I instead focused on the fact that each sibling occupied 204 cubic meters. While my parents — migrant field workers, warned us that the pesticides outside of our home could make us sick, I instead focused on how a pentachloralphenol compound compared to a Thiocarbomate compound. Or, how Chlorpyrifos chemically inhibits the enzyme acetyl cholinesterase.

My interest in engineering also developed throughout my academic career. In high school, I graduated from the Space & Engineering Academy with honors. At San Joaquin Delta College, I am a member of the Society of Hispanic Professional Engineers (SHPE), and a tutor for the Mathematics, Engineering, and Science Achievement Program (MESA) — tutoring college students in math, physics, and chemistry. I am also a Research Assistant in the Department of Chemistry at San Joaquin Delta College. I was awarded this position because I obtained a 96th percentile score on the American Chemical Society First Term Final Exam, and was one of two persons who earned an "A" grade in Chemistry 1A. This semester, I have founded a campus chapter of the American Chemical Society (ACS) and have been elected to serve as President of this organization.

Through learning chemistry and engineering-related curricula, completing ten college level courses while maintaining a 3.93 GPA, taking a leadership role in ACS and SHPE, and tutoring students within this discipline, my involvement has solidified my desire to obtain an undergraduate degree in chemical engineering.

As an undergraduate, I eagerly await potential internship and/or work study opportunities in a University of California laboratory to learn more about chemical engineering through experiments, research, and faculty interaction.

Aside from learning engineering theory, participating in engineering-related on-campus activities, my involvement has given me something I didn't expect: confidence. With this newfound confidence, I am certain I will continue to succeed academically and will make a significant contribution at my new University of California campus.

MY DRIVE TO SUCCEED
Rodrigo Tellez
(UC Berkeley)

The personal quality I am most proud of, and that relates to the person I am, is my drive to succeed. This quality is not something that has just happened overnight. This quality has evolved from before I entered kindergarten. When I was four years old, I was fascinated about a device that could function independently when I simply pressed a button: a calculator. As a four year-old I did not know that the functionality was simply an algorithm built into a circuit board. However, holding this calculator sparked a high level of curiosity in me. This curiosity grew when I learned that the type of individual who creates concepts like calculators is an engineer. It was at this point that I developed the desire to become an engineer. However, I knew that in order to become an engineer, it would require more than knowledge. It would require something internally. The moment I made up my mind to become an engineer, I also developed the drive to succeed.

The concept of becoming an engineer was not something organic to my life circumstances. Growing up on a migrant farm labor camp, I was not exposed to engineers. In fact, I had never met an engineer and only learned about the concept in school. However, that did not deter me from focusing on my goal. Starting in elementary school I challenged myself to participate in a rocket launch competition. I was eager to learn why some rockets propelled to a certain height while others failed, and how the center of gravity could impact performance. My desire to succeed remained throughout high school where I challenged myself to pursue a diploma from the Space & Engineering Academy at West High School. As the lead engineer in a robotics competition, I was tasked with programming an autonomous robot. My desire to succeed influenced my participation and yielded a first place victory for the Programming Challenge Award. My drive to succeed has continued to my current studies as a community college student. I have challenged myself to obtain the highest grades possible, to participate in engineering organizations, and to take advantage of rigorous engineering course offerings.

My drive to succeed will help me as an undergraduate student at a University of California campus. This drive will help me to remain focused, contribute significantly in classroom discussions, learn as many engineering theories and principles possible, and undertake engineering research and project-based opportunities. I am confident this drive will also assist me in dealing with obstacles, challenges, and the rigors of an engineering program of study. However, the most important and rewarding aspects of having a drive to succeed is that I will be the first in my family to earn a college degree. I am determined to make a valuable contribution to our society as an engineer.

YOU CANNOT RUN AWAY FROM INJUSTICE
Vanessa Fregoso
UCLA

As Junot Díaz wrote, "But if these years have taught me anything it is this: You can never run away. Not ever. The only way out is in." As a child, I realized that the only way to stop injustice is to understand the underlying contributing factors to problems, not overlook them. My sense of justice compelled me to participate in the changes that will ultimately improve the quality of life for all. By choosing to obtain my degree in Sociology and Social Welfare I will be passionately engaged in a field that sparks my interest and is central to my identity. In addition, this major will establish the foundation for an emphasis in Immigration Law and Civil Rights Law when I enroll in law school.

Early in my life I realized minorities are not fully advocated for by the law or by social norms. Growing up I first heard of the atrocities of the Bracero program through my grandfather's experiences as an exploited farm laborer. Appalled at how the system failed these hard working individuals, I realized the system was failing other marginalized groups. These experiences and lessons learned, empowered me to pursue a degree in Sociology and Social Welfare.

My field interests extend beyond a classroom through my social advocacy work. By continuously working alongside families through 800 extensive hours of non-profit efforts with the Coalition of Humane Immigrant Rights of Los Angeles, I gained real world insight on social issues and was able to identify and implement holistic solutions. With CHIRLA, the California Dream Network, People and Congregations Together, and Catholic Charities Immigration Legal Services of Stockton, I have participated in numerous social actions such as protests, rallies, and summits. I have spoken with elected officials, registered voters and hosted workshops to promote immigrant rights and services, as well as helped immigrants apply for eligible programs. As a result of my volunteer work and hands-on experience, I was awarded the 2013-2014 César Chávez Leadership Award Scholarship.

My advocacy work has enabled me to witness social movements and social theories in practice. These experiences have shown me deeper understandings of the *economical and societal effects of being a minority. I was able to apply post-colonial theories to many of the immigration discourses and witness the diaspora of those who have assimilated or been forced to assimilate. It is through this humbling and informative experience that I have become a more developed individual and have grown passionate about the social welfare and sociological solutions that can help those marginalized, all the while using these lessons as a foundation for my law career.*

The culmination of my academic studies, scholarly research, and significant community volunteerism has solidified my intent to pursue an undergraduate degree at a UC campus. I am eager to begin undergraduate studies in a research-based institution where I can further my education in order to continue helping the marginalized. I cannot help but believe it is my inherent duty to break down walls and build bridges for those struggling.

MY VIEW FROM THE TRAILER HOME
TO THE COUNTRY CLUB
Vanessa Fregoso
UCLA

For the first twelve years of my life, I lived in a harsh reality that evoked feelings of fear, shame, and powerlessness. I feared my parents would be deported, should an Immigration and Customs Enforcement (ICE) officer question their status. Whenever a strange car lingered near our home, my stomach turned upside down out of fear that my parents would be deported. Additionally, I was ashamed of where and how we lived. My family's small trailer home overlooked the fields where immigrant field workers hunched over fumigated crops, their backs to the sun and handkerchief-protected faces to the dirt.

Ironically, our trailer home was situated on a farm located directly next to a wealthy country club community. Their amenities, privileges, and lifestyle represented everything our family lacked. The luxury, two-story homes and mansions within the gated, upscale community were not only spacious, but the residents also had clean water and were not exposed to dangerous chemical pesticides. This experience caused me to question every aspect of my life, to analyze social class structure, and to try to understand the circumstances that led to my family's socioeconomic status.

Fortunately, my family went from living in a small trailer home to a modest, single-family home in Stockton, California. Although our home is by no means luxurious, we now have clean water, heating, and basic public utility services that most take for granted. Most importantly, my parents have become naturalized citizens, and no longer fear that ICE might revoke my parent's legal status and deport them. Still, the trauma of having lived in poverty and the fear of deportation never really escaped my mind.

It was not until I was a community college student that I fully understood and appreciated the brilliance of Gloria Anzaldua's statement, "The possibilities are numerous once we decide to act and not react." This became my truth when I became involved with the Coalition of Humane Immigrant Rights of Los Angeles, CHIRLA, an organization that helps our immigrant community. Anzaldua's statement resonated with me because I had learned through my social justice advocacy to act deliberately and with cause, rather than react emotionally. It is this personal strength, to act, that makes me proud and defines the person I am.

My work with CHIRLA empowered me to act in ways that benefit the marginalized, disenfranchised, and disadvantaged. I acted by participating in retreats, rallies, protests, and grassroots organizing. I registered naturalized citizens to vote with the California New Americans Vote Campaign, canvassing for support for certain ballot propositions, holding banner drops, and hosting various family workshops regarding legal updates and immigration rights.

My actions allowed me to identify an avenue through which I could help those around me to participate in authentic solutions regarding the social welfare of our society. I have been honored and privileged to serve my community and have learned the importance of leadership and applying myself through advocacy and education. The results of my action have positively impacted my community, and have influenced my decision to pursue higher education.

Using the TIN CASA Rubric (Chapter 7), Let's Analyze these Transfer Student Essays

Hopefully, in reading these four essays from two transfer students, you saw some of the key strategies outlined in this book.

For example, did you notice the consistent theme of *ganas*? I'm certain you are convinced (as were the Admissions Officers) that Rodrigo and Vanessa have the *ganas* to get the job done! We believe in them because their story resonated with us on multiple dimensions.

Tone. If we think in terms of tone, what did you feel? Was the tone fatalistic, or was it optimistic? Did these students convey an assertive sense of accomplishment, or did they sound conceited? Did we feel it was *their* story, written in their authentic voice? Rodrigo and Vanessa nailed it by demonstrating their obstacles but avoiding a demoralizing or victim tone. The overall tone for both was positive, inspirational, and optimistic.

Intellect. Clearly, these two superstars are intellectual dynamos. They referenced conceptual and technical details concerning their majors. They did not "dumb down" the topics to relate to a "lay person." They demonstrated their ease in which they would fit into a vibrant, intellectual community of scholars.

Narrative. We feel connected to Vanessa and Rodrigo's stories because they speak from a personal narrative: first person. We didn't feel a wall, disconnecting us from personally identifying with them. Their first person narrative invited us into their world.

Compelling Introduction. Vanessa and Rodrigo cleverly utilized the TIN CASA strategy for a Compelling Introduction. Vanessa used a quote, citing Junot Díaz. Rodrigo utilized the storytelling technique. He told us the story of how his interest in a simple calculator sparked his future desire to become an engineer.

Answer the Prompt. Did Rodrigo and Vanessa provide concrete examples to illustrate their intent to transfer? You can see how they methodically synthesized the way in which their experiences shaped their desire to pursue a particular major. It was not happenstance; they made it appear as though it evolved naturally.

Speak to Your Audience. Vanessa and Rodrigo appreciated that faculty and staff from within their academic major would be reading their

Personal Statements. Knowing this information helped them to speak to their audience. They methodically included technical references to convey their passion for the major. In addition, knowing that their words were not neutral and that their essay content was not apolitical, they carefully tailored their language.

Authenticity. Did these students convey Cultural Authenticity? We definitely have the sense Vanessa and Rodrigo have strong ties within their culture and communities. Not only did they speak to their cultural and socioeconomic upbringing, but they also brought it home by sharing their desire to give back to their communities. They nailed it!

Part Six

Putting it All Together - Sample Essays

Let's See Some Actual Essays!

With permission from students I've coached during the last five admission cycles, I am proud to present the following essays. While these students represent diverse experiences, interests, and backgrounds, they all utilized the methods outlined in this book. The selected essays represent a broad spectrum of campuses including the Ivy Leagues, Research I institutions, and public universities. In addition, the students responded to various prompts including the University of California prompts, as well as the older version and the newer version (Version 4) of the Common Application.

All of the students featured were admitted to *multiple* campuses. However, rather than listing all of the campuses each student was admitted, I chose one campus to highlight a representative sampling of the type of essay that yields admission to a particular university.

Please note that Harvard graduate Adan Acevedo graciously provided his essay for this book, although he was not part of my coaching practice. Gracias, Adan!

Finally, you will see that the following essays represent a wide range of writing abilities. Some of these students are native English writers who developed extensive essay-writing fluency through their AP or IB English coursework, while others were non-native English readers/writers, with somewhat limited proficiency. All in all, they "nailed" it!

MAKING MY OWN OPPORTUNITIES
Gabriella Herrera
(Harvard University)

Standing in the women's restroom at Stanford University Hospital, I laughed at the image of the girl staring back at me. I couldn't believe where I was and how far I had come from the agricultural valley of my small town of Tracy. The image I saw was a young Latina dressed in blue surgical scrubs with big brown eyes brimming with optimism. I felt proud as I clipped on my official Stanford badge, one that all the other doctors wear, and placed my cotton blue surgical cap on my head. In that moment I felt thankful and humbled I had been given a once-in-a-lifetime opportunity to pursue my passion: neuroscience.

This was my first day as an intern in the Neurodiagnostics Laboratory at Stanford University Hospital. I had just been instructed to change into a pair of scrubs so I could make my first trip to the operating room. After staring in the mirror for a few more seconds, I grabbed my clothes, gave thanks to *La Virgin de Guadalupe*, took a deep breath, and stepped out of the restroom a new person. In those few seconds of seeing myself in scrubs, I knew that all of my preparation had led me to this point.

This experience was overwhelming because it was both surprising and reaffirming. It surprised me because I could not have predicted this outcome 10 years ago, yet it was reaffirming because I have been preparing myself for this journey for at least 10 years. My goal is to become one of the first, if not the first, female Mexican-American neurosurgeons in the United States. Living in a small town that boasts the County Hay Growers Association, Tracy Shooting Supplies, one Walmart, and recently the grand opening of Tracy Rifle & Pistol, finding opportunities to pursue my interest in neuroscience is truly like finding a needle in a haystack.

Living in a small town like Tracy, aspiring to be a neurosurgeon, it would have been easier to concede my passion for neuroscience and resolve myself to identifying a more plausible interest. Fortunately, my love of science and my tenacious personality fueled me to figure out ways to create my own opportunities. Determined to reach my goal, I expanded my geographical radius and applied for summer internships all across the United States.

Beginning with the spring of my freshman year I figured out creative ways to identify specialized science-related programs for young students like myself. I wanted to gain knowledge about everything scientific so I began researching websites for Latino scientists like SACNAS, renowned technical institutions like MIT, Caltech, and Cornell, and neuroscience specific organizations like The Human BioMolecular Research Institute and Women in Neurosurgery (WINS). Although all those months of research and application preparation yielded only one interview, I knew I only needed one chance to prove myself.

When I received a phone call in spring of my sophomore year inviting me to interview for an internship at UC San Diego's School of Medicine, my family packed up the car and we drove more than 500 miles for this opportunity. Armed with my portfolio, optimism, and a genuine passion for science, my eagerness must have been evident as I was quickly notified of my acceptance into their program. That summer I worked with a team of 10 talented students researching the inhibition of the enzyme phosphofructokinase-1, for the purpose of identifying which substrate inhibits this protein.

The internship experience at UC San Diego only fueled my desire to learn more about science. Geared up and better prepared for the competitive world of internships, in my junior year I applied to five internship programs including MIT, Caltech, UC San Francisco, The National Institute of Health, and Stanford University. My prior internship experience, SAT scores, and AP coursework proved to be a successful combination. I received acceptance letters for 3 out of 5 programs, and chose Stanford because of their Neuroscience Institute.

The girl I saw in the mirror has come a long way, but still has a long way to go. There has never been a physician in the history of my family. Female neurosurgeons are still rare (less than 200 in the US today), and even more rare a Latina from the agricultural Central Valley of California. Aside from the fascinating scientific knowledge I've gained through summer internships, the technical knowledge acquired throughout my AP courses, possibly the most valuable lesson I've learned: if an opportunity doesn't exist, create one. I am confident this philosophy will be invaluable to me as I venture into the life of an undergraduate student — whether it is the study or neuroscience, mathematics, or physics.

THE BROOKE RUN
Adan Acevedo
(Harvard University)

The sun woke up around four forty in the morning every day (unless it was raining). Sometimes I woke up right as the sunlight crept into my window and pulled the little darkness I had under the covers away from me. My running shoes were always by the side of my bed, along with my shorts and a white T-shirt. As I run out of Jesus College in the morning, I'd see Cambridge starting to rub her eyes. Men, women, and children on bikes said quick "cheers!" as they flew by. Occasionally, I would see a runner coming the opposite way and we would give each other a mutual thumbs-up. My visit to England was years ahead of schedule.

Only a few weeks prior, I had been at home, turning off my computer late at night, going to bed, and trying to decide if I was hearing gunshots or fireworks as I dozed off. I would never go out to run at five in the morning in my hometown of Lennox, California. I knew the dangers that went with early-morning or late-night running. I have known of the gangs, drugs, and prostitution issues since I started going to school. Century Boulevard, although the exit for the Los Angeles International Airport, has an area that is infamous for being a center for prostitution. Lennox, a 1.1 square mile city, has twenty-seven graffiti gangs and fourteen much more dangerous gangs (like Lennox Trece [13] and others who steal and kill) that everyone is weary of. Teenage pregnancies come up every year, and I alone know at least fourteen or so individuals who have had children before the age of seventeen or had an abortion.

Searching lights shine through my windows every once in a while, and I can't help but hope that the man or woman running will not choose to break into my house. We have no alarm system and very few individuals in Lennox do. I have never really known the safety that other teenagers take for granted. In a town where less than two thousand people have graduated from high school, issues like these do not help the academic environment of students. The odds of a male Lennox student receiving financial aid from one of the best high schools in the city, of not dropping out, of not giving in to gang violence, of not giving in to the drugs or alcohol, of not fathering a child, and of taking full advantage of his opportunities are not exceedingly good.

Yet, I was in Cambridge debating immigration, the effects of globalization, my stance on humanitarian aid, and the right of a beetle on the Pump Court lawn to walk into my chicken and mango sandwich.

As sweat would begin to permeate my white T-shirt, I'd reach the Grantchester Meadows and run along the gorgeous walking path. I would then, after a trek of about a mile and a quarter, reach the memorial to Rupert Brooke. Then it would hit me. The town of Newton and Wittgenstein was just awakening. My ambition, love for philosophy, interest in politics, and thirst for the perfect poem or story were fed and shared by students from all over the world there. I'd run back to Cambridge from that memorial, in eager anticipation of the day's lectures and debates in my Politics in the Modern World class with an Oxford professor and my creative writing class with a published author. I not only had the historical town to attest to the importance of academia, but I had the fact that I was standing there as evidence of it. I decided I wanted to excel. I decided I wanted something better. It had just really hit me that my competitive nature and drive earned me opportunities that would leave any Lennox resident awestruck.

I drink Earl Grey tea regularly now. I walk with a different step. I run with a smile on my face. The world's stage will soon have new actors. I'm studying, reading, and practicing my lines so the transition into that lead role isn't too hard. However, I know I will never forget the city I came from and the issues that plague my community. Lennox gave me the few pearls it had to offer. I must give them back with interest. I will be back in Lennox in a few years before I hit the campaign trail, go into the classroom, excel in the laboratories, or push for legislation in the United States Senate. I will be prepared and I will drive for change in my community . . . and later, the world.

POLITICAL ASYLUM
AS A TRANSGENDER TEEN
Amber Escobar
(Mills College)

In September 2010, I challenged more than a belief or idea. I challenged a historically oppressive political, religious, and social structure. It was at this time — as a 15-year old, that I stood in front of an Immigration Judge, attorneys, and my family and gave testimony in support of my Foreign National petition to seek Political Asylum status as a Transgender individual. Although seeking Asylum is a costly, time-intensive, and emotionally draining process, I felt I did not have a choice to forego this opportunity or rescind my application for several reasons.

First, I could not return to my country of Mexico for fear of persecution to myself and my family. Secondly, I could not forego my plight to defend the rights of Transgender individuals like me, who wish to live a life with dignity, respect, and without fear. Lastly, I could not rescind my application because I am determined to pursue my passion for science and receive a college degree in the United States.

The country of Mexico is where I was born in 1996 as a male, as "Luis Escobar." This is a country where the religion of Catholicism is embedded into the politics, social norms, and "moral" code. It is *not* a country that embraces the LGBT community. It is a dangerous place for Transgender individuals like me who physically, emotionally, psychologically, and legally changed from "Luis" to "Amber." Because of my change, I could never return to my conservative town in Manzanillo, Mexico.

When I received my new status, I had a new decision to face: start my new life as a "normal" woman with no connection to being transgender, or to continue being an advocate for the Trans community. The answer was simple. I have a social responsibility to share my story. Although there are numerous advantages of staying out of the public eye, I am an active member of PFLAG (Parents, Families & Friends of Lesbians and Gays), I present at different universities, conduct televised interviews, and am featured in a documentary to help struggling Trans-Teens cope and "come out" to their families. My triumphant story has been motivating, and sometimes life-saving, to struggling transgender teens.

One of the unlikely, yet highly rewarding aspects of my transition has been my exposure to the medical field. From 2009 to present I've met with 10 doctors, learned about the physiological aspects of Estrogen therapy and Testosterone blockers, and learned how to navigate through the maze of private insurance. While this journey has been eye-opening, I have also learned about the sociological and psychological aspects of being Transgender. I have encountered stereotypes and other's views regarding socially constructed "moral codes" —how boys and girls should behave and feel. For example, although the recent release of the Diagnostic and Statistical Manual of Mental Disorders (the DSM) removed the term "Gender Identity Disorder" it replaced it with the term, "Gender Dysphoria." This new term has labeled the "condition" to be associated with clinically significant distress. I, and many others like me, do not feel "distressed." Terms like this have a stigmatizing effect, yet without an identifiable diagnosis, it would jeopardize access to mental and physical health care.

Therefore, it has become my goal to pursue undergraduate studies that combine biological sciences with a humanitarian approach. My goal is not to simply study human biology. I also want to learn how society, morals/ethics, and politics influence and shape the advancement of medicine. As an advocate for the Transgender community, I and am determined to advocate for patients who lack social, psychological, and medical support. I've had unique struggles being born in the wrong body, but the process of exploring my identity has been rewarding and liberating — making it something I wouldn't change even if I could.

UMMA, YOLISA, AND HANYEO
Sung-Eun Kim
(Princeton & Harvard)

When I was in the fifth grade I wore the hats of an *Umma, Yolisa, and Hanyeo*. In my native language of Korean, an *Umma* is a mother, a *Yolisa* is a cook, and a *Haneyo* is a housemaid. I was designated to serve in these roles because it was my duty, or *Uimu*. My parents worked multiple jobs, in odd hours, and it became my responsibility to ensure the household was maintained and my sister was fed. While it was frustrating and tiring to assume all of these roles at a young age, my body soon adapted and became mechanized to perform as an adult.

My typical day began before sunrise, frantically preparing breakfast for my younger sister and myself. After breakfast, I would expediently make the hour and a half round-trip walk to escort my sister to and from school. Once my sister was safely home, I would run to my employer's residence to cook and perform household duties. When the stars reappeared, I would finally be home, preparing dinner, and caring for my sister. It would not be until 11:00pm when I had time for myself.

While my body quickly adapted to this routine, my mind did not adapt so easily. I would often wake up to a soaked pillow, puffy eyes, and sadness in my heart. I yearned to be a young person, enjoying life. My heart squealed at the mention of a good novel, a visit to the zoo, or just a carefree afternoon. I frequently questioned why life was so challenging, and it became difficult to envision my future. I was perplexed with the irony of my life circumstances. After all, my family voyaged to America to escape a life of hardship.

In my new, foreign environment, I was unable to communicate with my peers. I grew resentful of my culture and was bullied by classmates. The students could not understand me, and were unfamiliar with the spectacle of a black-haired girl. I too remained skeptical of my classmates. I couldn't understand why they complained about not owning the newest laptop, when our family did not own a functioning computer. While my peers were enjoying their middleclass lives, our family bills were left unpaid, we struggled to find our next meal, and we were evicted from multiple homes.

For me, life was unbearable, but I knew it was also difficult for my parents. One day I saw the inhumane treatment my parents received due to their broken English and cultural differences. Witnessing this traumatic event reinforced what my parents have had to endure for my sister and me to have an opportunity for a better future. This negative experience was actually a positive catalyst. Putting aside my resentment, I realized I was needlessly feeling sorry for myself. My perspective shifted from my own personal hardship, to the compassion and appreciation I felt for my parent's sacrifices.

This new perspective dramatically influenced my actions and attitude. I became more responsible and more diligent in my role as *Umma, Yolisa,* and *Hanyeo.* Instead of resenting my responsibilities, I began to serve in this capacity with honor, dignity, and humility. I also began to view school differently. I realized it was not a place that stifled my abilities or rendered me to an inferior position, but an institution in which I would grow. Life, as hard as it was, was getting better as I discovered my passion for learning and my desire to change my future.

From this experience, I learned three valuable lessons. First, I learned that viewing my life situation from a position of gratitude would enhance everything in my world. Second, I learned that my shortcomings, suffering, and burden would allow me to grow into a stronger and more resilient person. Lastly, when I learned to appreciate the nuances in life, education became sacred. I had a sister that looked up to me, a family that depended on me, and an intellectual fire burning within myself that needed to be satisfied.

Education is an opportunity for a future —a privilege for those who value its presence. When I listen to a classroom lecture, I am oblivious to the scarce two hours of sleep I may have had the night before. Instead, I am intrigued by the origins of disease, calculus proofs, and microscopic life. It is with this mindset that I have been alive, achieving academic success while maintaining stability within my family. Fully embracing my *Uimu*, I feel it is my honor and duty to heal broken communities, and ultimately move the world. I have been an *Umma* since ten, a curious learner since birth, and I will be a student for life.

FROM FRUIT PICKER
TO AERONAUTICAL ENGINEER
Jesús Castillo
(Saint Mary's College)

On the road by 4:40am. Working every day from 5:00am until 7:00pm. Temperatures exceeding 100 degrees, without shade, fans, or cooling. These are the conditions in which I've worked the past four summers. As a farm worker I have picked every fruit and vegetable imaginable. Although we were given gloves, we breathed in pesticides and were required to remove pesticides from the rim of the fruits with our hands.

In addition to these conditions, our 10-person crew was aware of the fact our daily pay would be based on the number of fruit pieces we could pack in a single crate. Crate by crate, hour by hour, we worked ferociously to pack as many crates as possible. When sun set, we would split our commission between the ten of us.

These working conditions might sound sad or even frightening to most students at my high school. However, I am grateful I have had this opportunity. It is the positive mind set I developed over the years of working in the fields that I am most proud of. This background allowed me to see a future that I did not wish for myself or my future children. It made me determined to do well in school and has impacted my career aspiration.

Although I have not had many resources to prepare me for conceptual physics or calculus, my positive mindset and optimistic attitude have kept me on track and focused. I believe this quality of a positive mindset is going to propel me beyond an undergraduate degree — toward contributing in a significant way in the field of engineering.

BOTOX, MOYA-MOYA, AND CRAINIOTOMIES
Gabriella Herrera
(Stanford University: Early Action)

"Time out. Dr. Li, Surgeon. Dr. Nguyen, Interoptive Monitoring. Chuck, Circulating Nurse. Starting incision. Time marked is 9:03am."

As the surgeon begins, the room fills with the unmistakable smell of burnt skin. "Bzzzzzzzz." The buzzing sounds as the surgeon begins to drill through the skull. The nurse hands the surgeon the surgical scissors to cut through the meninges. "OK, let's get an image up." The brain surgery begins . . .

Many of my days as an intern in the Neurodiagnostics Laboratory at Stanford University Hospital began like this. I spent eight weeks working on my own research as well as observing MCA/ECA bypass surgery, aneurysm clippings, brain tumor removal, Moya-Moya bypass surgery, arteriovenous malformation bypass surgery, and awake craniotomies. Every day was a new journey into the neuroscience world, and every day I could see myself more clearly in my desired profession — a neurosurgeon.

On one of the occasions when I accompanied the Principal Investigator, Dr. Jaime Lopez, on his clinical rounds, a patient came into the lab to receive his annual botox shots. "Botox?" I thought. Dr. Lopez explained that this patient had hyperactive muscles, and the botox was used to relax these muscles. It was extremely humbling when the patient arrived, and I saw his deformed body. His jaw, legs, and arms were stiff and immovable. I was taken by the fact that doctors and scientists had found a method to help this patient — one who is unable to eat, move, or function properly without family aid and whose condition has so affected their family members. After observing the treatment, I was humbled by how much a physician can help another person's quality of life. This taught me the great potential we all have to help those around us, and improve other people's lives.

I have always known that I would be in a medical profession, but this experience solidified my belief that I will become a neurosurgeon. I knew at a very young age that I wanted to be a member of *Los Médicos Voladores* or the "Flying Doctors." *Los Médicos Voladores* travel into remote villages in Mexico and Central America providing free medical aid to those who cannot afford their services. As a neurosurgeon I would be able to help those from impoverished towns like Tijuana, B.C., -- where my biological father and most of my Herrera family live.

I believe we have all been given unique gifts and talents but we don't often use them for the greater good. The experience I had at Stanford will remain in my mind throughout my college years. This experience will continue to motivate me so that one day I will be that neurologist advancing the quality of life for others.

MY DRIVE TO SUCCEED
Rodrigo Tellez
(UC Berkeley)
Regents' & Chancellor's Scholar
2014 Recipient Dream America Scholarship
Featured on the "Katie Couric Show"

The personal quality I am most proud of, and that relates to the person I am, is my drive to succeed. This quality is not something that has just happened overnight. This quality has evolved from before I entered kindergarten. When I was four years old, I was fascinated about a device that could function independently when I simply pressed a button: a calculator. As a four year-old I did not know that the functionality was simply an algorithm built into a circuit board. However, holding this calculator sparked a high level of curiosity in me. This curiosity grew when I learned that the type of individual who creates concepts like calculators is an engineer.

It was at this point that I developed the desire to become an engineer. However, I knew that in order to become an engineer, it would require more than knowledge. It would require something internally. The moment I made up my mind to become an engineer, I also developed the drive to succeed.

The concept of becoming an engineer was not something organic to my life circumstances. Growing up on a migrant farm labor camp, I was not exposed to engineers. In fact, I had never met an engineer and only learned about the concept in school. However, that did not deter me from focusing on my goal. Starting in elementary school I challenged myself to participate in a rocket launch competition. I was eager to learn why some rockets propelled to a certain height while others failed, and how the center of gravity could impact performance.

My desire to succeed remained throughout high school where I challenged myself to pursue a diploma from the Space & Engineering Academy at West High School. As the lead engineer in a robotics competition, I was tasked with programming an autonomous robot. My desire to succeed influenced my participation and yielded a first place victory for the Programming Challenge Award. I have challenged myself to obtain the highest grades possible, to participate in engineering organizations, and to take advantage of rigorous engineering course offerings.

My drive to succeed will help me as an undergraduate student at a University of California campus. This drive will help me to remain focused, contribute significantly in classroom discussions, learn as many engineering theories and principles possible, and undertake engineering research and project-based opportunities. I am confident this drive will also assist me in dealing with obstacles, challenges, and the rigors of an engineering program of study.

However, the most important and rewarding aspects of having a drive to succeed is that I will be the first in my family to earn a college degree. I am determined to make a valuable contribution to our society as an engineer.

SCIENCE WITHOUT HUMANITY
Arianna Fernandez
(UC Berkeley)

My background is central to my identity and can be summarized by two impactful statements. Each statement represents how I perceive my world, and has profoundly influenced my dreams and aspirations. One part of my background that is central to my identity can be described in the quote by Alex Haley: *"The family is link to our past, bridge to our future."* As a Latina, my family holds a significant value in my life. My family has impacted my values, philosophy, and life goals, and has built the bridge to my future academic and life success. For example, my family taught me the value of hard work, high moral ethics, and to never accept "average" but to strive for exceptional. These values have become a bridge toward opportunity. It is these values that inspired me and sustained me through a challenging four years of high school.

The other part of my background that has shaped my identity is guided by one of the seven deadly sins by Mahatma Gandhi, "*Science without Humanity.*" I appreciate Gandhi's understanding of how we have progressed and advanced scientifically through technology, yet remain in the past with regard to inequity and injustice. I witnessed "Science without Humanity" during my father's battle with brain cancer. For several years I saw him suffer repeatedly through grand mal seizures, pain, and endless medication. Because our family is low-income, we could not afford specialty care. When you suffer in poverty, "humanity" is often a foreign concept.

Consequently, my father received sub-par care such as being denied approval for a costly CT Scan. After several years, and three unnecessary open-heart surgeries, the physicians finally realized my father had a brain tumor. Through this ordeal, our family struggled financially and emotionally, yet we learned important skills like sharing responsibility, patience, and we developed an immense amount of compassion.

The other outcome of this experience was the impact it made on my desire to pursue a career in medicine. This experience helped me envision how I might provide medical care for others in a humane way. This not only changed my perspective and general outlook on life, but made me more mature, opened my eyes to the healthcare industry, and prepared for a rigorous pathway to college.

Hungry to learn every aspect of the medical field, I applied and was accepted to the Stanford Medical Youth and Science Program (SMYSP). This summer experience allowed me to thoroughly explore medicine. I attended lectures from the Deans of Stanford Medical School, learned Human Anatomy, and worked at Stanford Medical Hospital in a 5-week internship.

During my internship I examined Cadavers, witnessed surgeries, and shadowed physicians. The culmination of my experiences and passion for the pursuit of sciences, significantly guides my pathway to college.

My background has led to a passion for science, compassion and human dignity for others, and the will to succeed. This background is central to my identity because it has impacted my academic pursuits, my passion for biological sciences, and instilled in me the drive to make a difference in the larger "world." Although I have had many struggles, I am very appreciative my struggles led to opportunities for growth and learning. It is this unique perspective that will shine bright as I begin my undergraduate studies.

MY FIGHTING SPIRIT: A TKO
Christina Silva
(UC Irvine & UC Riverside)

Recently, the Light Middleweight boxer Santos Saúl Álvarez Barragán (aka "Canelo") spoke about his upcoming fight with Floyd Mayweather, Jr. He said, *"This will be a tough physical fight, but I feel I have a lot of advantages. I am working on the things I can take advantage of."* His words resonate with me because in my spirit I am also a fighter. Although I do not fight in a boxing ring, I have symbolically fought against many obstacles within my lifetime.

Growing up, I encountered many "blows" in the form of financial and academic challenges. While I realized I could not control many of the circumstances imposed upon me, I also realized there were "things I can take advantage of." These are my fighting words. In understanding this important concept, I have become a champion in confronting my opponent (my obstacles), understanding how to strategically maneuver, and how to ultimately "win."

Financially, our family has endured poverty our entire lifetime. My father is the sole provider for our family of six, and money has always been scarce. I resolved to concede expectations for lavish gifts at Christmas time or my birthday, and learned to prioritize my expenditures. As a result I have become very creative in identifying ways to save money. Growing up in poverty led me to develop coping skills, how discern between wants and needs, and to prioritize my expenses. Poverty was a swift left jab, but I swiftly counter punched and won this round.

Having won that round, I confronted another obstacle: academics. Academically, I am a first generation college student. My father was a "cholo" in the streets of East Los Angeles and dropped out of high school in the ninth grade. My mother also dropped out of high school. While this was discouraging, I realized I had the tools to shape my future and set my own goals. I enrolled and thrived in rigorous courses such as AP Biology, AP Calculus, Human Anatomy and a Chemistry course at UC Riverside. These foundational courses were fascinating to me, and provided me with validation that I could thrive in a science-related academic curriculum. My newfound knowledge helped me throw short hooks, a long jab, and defeat the challenge of rigorous academics.

Like Canelo, I have been the underdog with a fighting spirit. I have looked at my opponent, square in the eyes, and did not shy away. Rather than succumbing to defeat, or conceding life, my many obstacles have positively influenced my goals, decisions, and actions. The culmination of how I have responded to these circumstances has made me a stronger person.

As I look ahead to my life as an undergraduate student, I am prepared to tackle any unforeseen challenges and to succeed. My resilience, strength, and commitment to my educational goals will render me undefeated. Moving forward, I am no longer an unprepared fighter. I am a skilled pugilist, equipped with the tools, strategies, and spirit to triumph. As the great Muhammad Ali once said, "If my mind can conceive it, and my heart can believe it - then I can achieve it."

I CAN'T SHAKE MY HIPS LIKE THAT!
Rafael Garibay
(UCLA)

When the automatic door opened and a fresh cadaver was wheeled in on a gurney, I was both fascinated and mortified. I was fascinated at concepts I was learning at Stanford Hospital; viewing human anatomy and learning physiological processes. However, I was mortified that I would be asked to explain to my peers the importance of the left ventricle pumping blood to the rest of the body at a much higher pressure than any other heart chamber.

When the gurney stopped in front of me, I inhaled embalming fluids. For a moment I too wished I had a preserving agent that would freeze time and take me back to my high school classroom. At Delhi High School, I had the classroom ritual and process down to a science. I could present at any time, to my peers, without hesitation or fear. However, this was not Delhi High School, and these were not my peers. I was surrounded by a group of twenty-four intelligent scholars, medical school staff, and physicians. I knew this very moment would quickly define my transition from childhood and my high school experience, to adulthood and my road to undergraduate studies.

Prior to my arrival at Stanford's five-week Medical Youth Science Program, I was confident and assured in my intellectual abilities. After settling in, I began to feel hesitant about approaching my peers. I thought, "They must be bright. They probably have perfect SAT scores." I felt my movements were meticulously gauged with scholarly expectations, so I was careful not to say too much, or too little. These assumptions remained with me until we conducted our first "Ice Breakers" exercise. It wasn't until this summer opportunity that I felt I was in my academic element. Slowly, I began my transition from childhood to adulthood.

One of the highlights of the program and an event that contributed to my transition was our Bollywood workshop. Initially, I felt awkward and afraid I would appear ridiculous in front of my new friends. I was used to dancing to Latino music like *norteño, banda, cumbia, and salsa.* I attempted to behave casually so I was not noticed. Suddenly, I was asked to come dance but I smiled and said, "Oh, no. I don't know how to shake my hips like that!" My friend said, "You could do it!" and pulled me up. To my surprise, I found myself loving the rapid rhythm of Hindi music as I moved my body with speed until the need to catch my breath. Gradually, I found the comfort that helped me share my perspectives despite their backgrounds, and admire diversity regardless of differences.

This new environment fostered my curiosity and amplified my interpersonal abilities. I welcomed an incredibly diverse group of students from various nationalities and ethnicities that pushed me out of my comfort zone. This dynamic helped me mature as an individual and sharpen my analytical skills as I learned about different religions, cultures, language, and philosophy. My sense of leadership contributed greatly in dynamics of working with others in keeping group work on topic and focused. I learned the ability to combine my intellect with compassion about health and social causes that affect underserved Americans.

As I reflect on my journey at the Stanford Medical Youth Science Program, I am proud I represented my family, school, and community. I am a reshaped individual; vastly different from the timid man who stepped foot on Stanford's campus. My teachers witnessed a growth because I now comprehend the importance of being globally conscious to help others. Prior to my participation in SMYSP I was somewhat reserved and cautious. Fortunately, the program was the catalyst for my transition and served as the platform that launched an apprehensive young man to a new level of maturity, awareness, and intellect. After five memorable weeks, I am a young man diving into the life of adulthood.

MI ABUELITA – THE SUPERHERO
Victoria Arias
(UC Merced)

As a little girl, I imagined that *mi abuelita* — my grandmother, was a superhero. I heard countless stories of *abuelita's* super powers to heal scorpion stings, treat arthritis, cure colic, and alleviate anxiety with medicinal plants and herbs. In her *rancho* in *Zapotitlán*, national strip chain pharmacies and online pharmaceutical shopping were nonexistent.

Instead, *abuelita* relied on natural resources to gather, mix, and create necessary remedies for her twelve children. To my father, she would say, "*Hijo de maguey, mecate,*" as she gently applied *sabila* — an aloe extract to his cuts and burns. "*Mecate* is made from the fibers of the plant, *maguey*" she explained. "You and I are made out of the same stuff. You inherit my traits and follow in my steps."

After visiting my superhero in her *rancho* when I was ten, I finally understood why her powers were so invaluable. As a *hierbera*, or herbalist, *abuelita* was practicing a form of indigenous culture passed down through the oral tradition. This is the way my family — *La Familia Arias*, has lived for centuries. And, it was not until my father immigrated to the United States that we would experience modern medicine.

This background is central to my identity for many reasons. First, the historical account of my ancestor's background and journey from the dirt-and-gravel hills of *Zapotitlán* to the illuminated asphalt roads of Central California inspires me. It is this story that drives me to preserve the Arias tradition. However, as part of a new generation, my background has influenced my quest for higher education. Soon, I will become the first graduate-level college recipient in my family's history.

While *mi abuelita* used the juice of cactus as a cleansing agent, I will now be able to study how the alkaloid hordenine and tyramine have antiseptic properties due to their phenolic function. The concepts I've learned in AP Chemistry, AP Biology, AP Physics, and AP Calculus have provided a very basic foundation, or starting point of knowledge. However, as I begin my undergraduate studies, I will have the privilege of learning more advanced concepts such as structures of organic molecules, atomic and molecular structure, organic chemistry, and mathematical models for chemistry.

As I venture onto my new undergraduate campus, I will bring with me an inquisitive nature, intellectual curiosity, as well as reverence for my cultural ties. I strongly believe my sense of community, devotion to care for others, and cultural background will help me to remain focused and thrive in a rigorous chemistry program. As my *abuelita* believed, I inherited her traits and will follow in her steps. As an undergraduate student pursuing the disciplines of Chemistry and Pharmacy, I will honor *mi abuelita* by becoming a modern day superhero — *una hierbera*.

TINKERING WITH TOYS & BECOMING AN ENGINEER
Jesús Castillo
(UC Riverside)

"An optimist will tell you the glass is half-full; the pessimist, half-empty; and the engineer will tell you the glass is twice the size it needs to be." This may sound humorous, but this is my world: the world of an engineer. In my world, terms

like stress-strength interference, probabilistic design, systems reliability, and fatigue under random loading, are fascinating concepts. To my friends and relatives these terms sound unusual and boring.

As a very young boy, mechanical design has always been second-nature to me. I had an unusual interest in mechanical objects such as cars, airplanes, boats, and other machines. Whether it was building a Lego structure, or helping my teacher assemble a new desk, the practical aspect of mechanical engineering was always "common sense" to me. It was not until middle school that I began to participate in hands-on mechanical engineering projects.

One project in particular was building a rocket. In this project I learned that with certain impulse (collapse: Force x time) you would automatically, with some calculations, find the distance where the rocket stops before descending back down. This project enabled me to think more about science and its work. Another project was in conceptual physics where I built a wooden guitar with fish lines as strings. The project was to detect how many hertz and at what tension each string would send waves at a fast pace. In this sound wave project I identified and applied concepts of physics while playing the guitar.

Through these practical hands-on projects, I began to put together how the theoretical concepts in my coursework could be applied to practical aspects. It was amazing to me how concepts like conceptual physics, pre-calculus, and chemistry can be a "key" to unlocking very practical human issues. It was at this point I realized my interest in mechanical engineering could become a career.

While mechanical engineering is a large part of my world, I cannot overlook the other part of my world that has influenced who I am and what I wish to become. Growing up in Patterson, California — a rural farming community — mechanical engineering was not a thought in my mind.

My parents and I are migrant field workers. My stepfather only finished the 2nd grade, and my mother was fortunate to get to the 8th grade. We pick crops like tomatoes, peaches, and apricots. We have always lived in very small and humble conditions, conveniently close to seasonal crops. This world is comprised of rising early, working hard, and trying to make ends meet while studying and trying to earn high marks. Having lived and worked in migrant farm communities, it is quite unique that I will become the first person in my family to go to college.

I believe the combination of my worlds — my love of engineering and my migrant farm worker background, will lead me to success as an undergraduate. My work in the fields has given me the strength to persevere while my love of engineering will keep me focused and engaged. The combination of these worlds will bring a unique perspective to my future undergraduate campus.

THE TURTLE TRANSFORMED
Rosalyn Lozano
UC San Diego (Political Science)

My older sister Ulani smiles adoringly, pats me on the back and says, "You have a likeable personality. People *like* you." I laugh when she says this because I was not always characterized this way. Instead, I recall the many years when I did not have such a "likeable" personality and instead behaved like a shy turtle.

Like a turtle, I preferred to be alone, and would rarely poke my head out for fear of gaining attention. As a significantly overweight young girl, my gut wrenched when I heard the muffled nickname, "Rolls-alynn." Although the name-calling was hurtful, I was most upset about being the center of attention. I disliked how people laughed at me. As a young girl, this experience impacted my self-image and self-esteem.

Like a turtle, I would retreat — pulling my legs and head into my shell for protection, and folding my neck to the side. However, the shy turtle personality did not suit me. Inside of me, there was a strong, high-spirited, energetic, and positive person longing to emerge. I became determined to break out of my protective, weathered, turtle shell.

The break occurred in middle school — surprising my family, peers, relatives, and neighborhood. It was at that time I realized that my protective shell was not serving me well and was standing in the way of my true expressive personality. It was also preventing me from accomplishing the many academic and social goals I had set for myself.

Slowly, I began disintegrating my keratinous scutes, one by one, breaking down my carapace. My cold blooded physiology began to warm. As my top shell began to diminish, I noticed how positively my peers perceived, responded, and interacted with me. I had a fresh start. I learned that my smile best represented my spirit, and that it was contagious. My newly emerged personality helped me develop new acquaintances.

As my shell shed, I grew a cadre of friends. My newfound confidence, perpetual smile, and funny disposition attracted new friends with hundreds of students. My newfound confidence also impacted my grades. I went from 2.0's-3.0 GPA to having my first 4.0. I went on to become the Salutatorian of the class of 2010.

While I was developing my communication skills, I also became involved in programs like the Ivy League Project, interned at Assembly Member Henry T. Perea's Office, joined the Young Legislators Program, joined various clubs/ Programs and donated approximately 100-150 hours of community service. I also learned that in order to accomplish my goals, I couldn't be shy in asking others for help. I sought admission expertise from Quetzal Mama, asked professionals and school administrators to review my college applications, and gathered a committee for reviewing my personal statements.

I've learned that you can be out going, because being shy is a disadvantage. The traits that I have obtained can give me confidence to approach any issue I face on a college campus. I will be going out for clubs and community service projects. I will be willing to try new adventures, meet new people, study hard in college.

My personality has grown for the better. I've learned through time that many individuals in the world will try to tear you down, with one rude comment after another. But in my case I seeped through the bullies hands and surrounded myself with positive people who are not judging me.

Today, I am a different person. I have broken the barriers that were set in front of me. While I no longer refer to myself as a shy turtle, I retained some of my previous turtle-like qualities such as having a tough shell. I am now strong and able to deal with the odds and ends that life throws at me. The turtle is gone.

FROM TRAJEDY TO TRIUMPH
Daniel Morataya
(UC Santa Barbara)

On the night after a competition for my robotics team, a horrible thing happened. On the way back to our campus, a car had crashed into the back of our teacher's truck. The truck was barely damaged, and no one was hurt. However, our delicate thousand-dollar robots were severely mangled. So, my team had to rebuild them from scratch. We had to raise money to buy new parts, and we had to redesign the robot to refurbish what we could not afford to replace. After weeks of rebuilding and perseverance, we finally had our robots working. Our robots were better than ever.

Watching my team's robot being lifted and driven away is a difficult feeling to explain. First, it is a massive rush of joy to work on the robots. Spending three days every week, programming, designing and testing different parts for our robot, and re-working so that it runs optimally at full functionality, has given me so much. All of the design challenges we've faced have taught me how to think through a problem in order to find the solution.

Working with my team of six has taught me how to manage a good team. But most of all, it has taught me how to keep working through all the setbacks that appear. From realizing we used the wrong gear ratios, to having to repair the robot after the car accident, we had to overcome these obstacles. We moved past these obstacles to win 11 prizes in the four years I've been a member.

From the robot catastrophe, I learned many things. First, I learned that no matter how frustrating the problem I face, it is worth it to persevere through completion. Second, I learned to seek help from others versus trying to resolve (and in this case, repair) everything independently. Finally, I learned that there is always room for improvement and that sometimes when we reconfigure something — whether a robot or a mathematical formula, it may result in a superior outcome.

When I leave West High School's Space & Engineering Academy, I'll continue to work hard. I may be moving on, but I am looking forward to each and every challenge. Whether it is pulling an "all-nighter" studying for a midterm in Differential Equations, or conducting research for a physics project, I am ready for the many challenges I will encounter at a University of California campus.

MUSIC TAUGHT ME TO IMPROVISE
Janet Camacho
(UC Santa Cruz)

I was shaking, panicking and fearful. All I could think was *"Don't mess up!"* Although my feelings were overwhelming, the moment I started singing in front of an audience, they disappeared. Music has given me confidence in myself that I wouldn't have otherwise. I used to shy away from a lot things before. Music has taught me how to give it my all and to work hard for something that I really want.

Ever since I was a toddler I would entertain my parents and family as they watched me play tunes on a miniature keyboard. While I had the potential to play the piano, my parents could not afford to put me through lessons. Growing up I was involved in other activities like sports and choirs, yet I would not give up on piano. I took all of the resources I could find and taught myself how to play the piano. Since elementary school I would take what little I learned and put it to practice at home.

Eventually, I gained more knowledge in music. It wasn't until October of 2011 that I took my first piano lesson. My piano teacher was astonished that I could play at an advanced level without ever having taken lessons, or without any other resources.

While I do enjoy playing piano, I don't use my talent just for fun. I also sing to senior citizens as part of my church. It is a humbling experience to do so as they are joyful when I perform for them. I also use my talent for kids in elementary school as I am a teacher's aide. As a teacher's aide in music class I encourage students to appreciate music. It is exciting to see the students experience music and enjoy it as I do. Since I never had the opportunity to take piano lessons growing up, I decided that I would give lessons to those kids who wanted to learn piano but could not afford the cost of studio instruction. In teaching piano I have learned many qualities such as patience and tenacity.

Music has also taught me how to improvise. For example, if I mess up somewhere in life I always think of how I would improvise in music and make things better. I try to apply this same concept into my life practice. For example, my grades were not so great my first few years of high school. However, I improvised through adapting various strategies, which resulted in higher grades. Having successfully improvised, I was able to receive recognition for maintaining a GPA of 3.0 and above.

My musical ability is what I am most proud of. From this ability, I have acquired many qualities that have helped better myself academically and socially. I have learned to improvise when necessary, and to push forward to do my best. I am looking forward to composing my under-graduate repertoire at a University of California campus, and taking a bow upon my commencement.

THE BIG BROWN *ELEFANTÉ* IN THE ROOM
Carlos Ocampo
(University of Southern California)

"Why are you dressed like that Carlos?" asked my classmate Eddie when our teacher wasn't looking. He was wondering why I was wearing rabbit pelt, moccasins, a beaded necklace with abalone shell, and red dye face painting. There I stood on the blacktop, standing out amongst the hundreds of other students wearing "traditional" pioneer clothing such as overalls for the boys and cotton blouses and dresses for the girls.

It was "Pioneer Week" at our school — an event that is one of the highlights and a rite of passage for fourth graders at Saint Anthony's Elementary School. Although the class assignment was to dress up as a typical pioneer during the mid 1850's, it never occurred to me *not* to dress up as a Native American. Because I chose to represent the Native American tribes that existed during this era, my peers looked at me in bewilderment.

My clothing and my presence on the black top was personal to me. My ancestors descend from the *Caxcanes* Indians of *Juchipila* and *Nochistlán* in southern Zacatecas, as well as the Yaqui Indians of Sonora and the current American southwest. Although it was clear my teacher was visually aware of my presence, she did not comment or initiate a dialogue about my attire. In retrospect, she was probably fearful I would be ostracized had she approached me.

I was the big brown elephant in the room. After what seemed like hours (although it was probably only 5 or 10 minutes), my classmate's attitude changed from bewilderment to sincere curiosity. Frances was the first student who began asking me about my necklace. I explained that the necklace was designed and hand-made specifically for me, by a member of the *Obispeño* Northern Chumash tribe. I proudly explained that the red trade beads and shell beads came when the white people arrived in California, and that the abalone is used because it represents protection. After a while, many students were surrounding me and asking me questions about my clothing and about my Native American ancestry.

This experience was significant to me because it was the starting point that has created, shaped, and established my sense of personal identity today. While I am not a rebel by definition, this experience taught me to take a risk, be genuine, and listen to my instincts. Since that time I have continued to listen to my instincts and take risks with the goal of helping others to learn about multiple perspectives.

For example, because I aspire to be a screenwriter and because there are few positive images of Latinos in the mainstream media, I decided to create my own documentary film. In spring 2009 I began an independent documentary entitled, "Chicano Identity." I conceptualized the topic, created story boards, and organized the sequencing. I targeted a select group of prominent individuals I felt exemplify Chicano identity, including Dolores Huerta, Dr. Hayes-Bautista, John Trasviña (Assistant Secretary for Fair Housing & Equal Opportunity), Dr. Leo Chavez (Professor of Anthropology, UC Irvine), Astronaut José Hernandez, and CNN correspondent Soledad O'Brien.

I travelled to meet with these individuals and began filming, editing segments, and finalizing my introduction and final scene. I created this film with young students as my target audience. My goal was to present another side of Latino identity through the medium of film; to counter the negative messages predominantly portrayed in mainstream media. I am hopeful that another young Chicano or Chicana may access my film and develop his or her own sense of positive identity.

Since the Pioneer Days experience, I continue to take risks, challenge the mainstream, and bring a unique perspective to all of my endeavors. It is this sense of unique and non-traditional identity that I would also bring to my future university campus.

ESTAMOS RICOS DE AMOR
José Luis Fausto
(Willamette University)

"*Estamos ricos de amor.*" That is a saying my mother chimed whenever my siblings and I would ask her why we did not have money. This phrase translates to, "We are rich, rich of love." The richness she referred to was not monetary wealth; it was the emotional bond we held toward each other, as well as the love we had for those around us. It also represents a conviction that has shaped my dreams and aspirations. It represents the love I have for pursuing higher education and wanting to better my life. My mother was not naïve and did not have her head in the clouds, as they say. In fact, her philosophy in life was really brilliant. She knew that our mind often has greater power over the physical, and to appreciate the concept of love in order to enable us to achieve our goals.

This phrase has been with our family for decades. When my family emigrated from Mexico to the United States, I was only four years old. Although my family had material wealth in Mexico (relative to others), they wanted a better life for me and my siblings. It was the love they felt, being "*ricos de amor*," that compelled them to take a chance and leave it all behind. Fortunately for me and my siblings, their love was strong enough to provide us with a better education. My parents have supported me in every decision I have made and have also pushed me to join sports, and to give back to my community. Thanks to my parents, their leadership skills were passed down to me. They push me to become educated and have allowed me to become independent and responsible.

As an independent person making my own academic decisions, I enrolled in Advance Placement courses instead of opting for a less challenging curriculum. I have been featured numerous times in the East Union Honor Roll and currently hold a 3.6 grade point average making me part of the top 10% of my class. The leadership skills passed down to me encouraged me to enroll in Student Leadership to improve my skills as well as making the campus more inclusive of all students.

Being rich is not necessarily someone with a lot of money. It is someone who loves themselves as they love those around them. I'm proud to have inherited the "Fausto" surname, and the family reverence to "love." The love they have instilled in me is an important principle that will guide my undergraduate pursuits, and my lifelong career goals.

MANUAL LABORER TO UNIVERSITY RESEARCHER
Michelle Benavidez
(Yale)

In summer of 2013, I walked onto UC San Francisco's Fresno State campus. I was wide-eyed, nervous, but eager to begin my clinical research. Participating in UCSF's Biomedical and Health Sciences Internship was a far cry from my standard summer routine as a manual laborer for my father's small lawn-mowing business.

Typically, my summers are filled with determining ground saturation levels for herbicides and organic fertilizers. However, this summer my focus was determining the acculturation level of first-generation Mexican immigrants using the Acculturation Rating Scale for Mexican Americans II (ARSMA). Slowly, I put away my industrial level, cowhide leather gloves, and submerged myself in Scale Descriptors, Psychometric Properties, Conceptual and Theoretical Structure.

Although I am grateful I can help my family earn additional income, departing from my standard summer routine was the transition I had been anticipating. While I was accustomed to excelling in high school, I was now amongst scholars and the expectations were significantly higher. I quickly learned the laboratory standards of being punctual, attending to minute details, and being prepared. I also learned that in a research environment, my work is not conducted independently — my team relied on each member's contribution. Each team member's task was equally important, and our cumulative research would determine the quality of our research paper. Learning these new skills and adapting to this new environment was part of my transition from childhood to adulthood.

My successful transition from high school student to university researcher was in large part influenced by my parents. My parents have always envisioned a better life for me and have made many sacrifices to help me accomplish my academic goals. Although both my parents received only a middle school education, they have taught me the most important lessons about academia. They taught me the value of hard work, dedication, and determination. These values have shaped my academic career, influenced my performance in my internship program, and made me a stronger person. I am grateful I was able to use the valuable skills my parents taught me to successfully transition from childhood to adulthood.

My transition from high school student to university researcher was also marked by my environment growing up. The city of Fresno is teaming with diversity — the influence of many cultural groups makes it an intriguing heterogeneous community. Living in a diverse community, and closely identifying with my Mexican-American heritage, has provided me with a wider world perspective and a greater understanding of people. This unique perspective has helped me grow as a student, and directly impacted my perspective within my research. I believe my unique environment growing up helped me to thrive during my transition in the summer research program.

The combined influences and experiences — from my parent's wisdom, to my unique community environment, helped me to successfully transition from a high school student to a university researcher. During my summer internship I grew in many ways. I learned how it felt to be part of a team, to work amongst scholars, and to perform to the best of my abilities. However, the most important factor that influenced my transition this summer was realizing who I am and where I am going. As the daughter of immigrant, middle school educated, hard working parents, I will soon begin my undergraduate studies at a four-year university. I am looking forward to transitioning into the world of an undergraduate student — where I will again be wide-eyed, nervous, but eager.

Glossary

ACT – The American College Testing (ACT) examination tests students in English, mathematics, reading, and science. There is also an optional 30-minute essay portion. Colleges use the ACT as an assessment tool for admission consideration. Students may take this examination in lieu of or in addition to the SAT.

Advanced Placement (or "AP") – These are high school classes designated as college preparatory and are weighted for GPA and class ranking purposes. There are corresponding AP examinations administered by the College Board for various subject matters (such as English, biology, etc.).

Analogy – An analogy is a literary device that compares and contrasts two dissimilar things by establishing a relationship based on similarities. It is a highly effective persuasive-writing technique used in Personal Statements.

College Admissions Coach – often referred to as a "Consultant." Generally, an individual with expert and specialized knowledge who provides guidance to students seeking admission to selective colleges.

Colloquialism – Informal terms or phrases that are typically used within a particular region or organization. See Colloquialisms, Euphemisms, and Slang, in Chapter 11, "Mistake No. 10" in *Top 10 Mistakes Students Make*.

215

Common Application – The Common Application is an online application used by more than 500 private universities and colleges in the US. A student completes one "common" application that can be sent to multiple universities. Currently the Common App requires one 650-word Personal Statement (and some campuses require additional supplemental essays).

Cultural Authenticity – Cultural Authenticity refers to the quality a student possesses that represents positive, strong, and consistent affiliation within a cultural group. This quality is based on authentic life experiences within the culture and examples may include religion, politics, language, traditions, and historical knowledge. See Chapter 7, *TIN CASA*.

Descriptive Language – This is language that paints a picture for your reader by utilizing specific details and technical terms. Adjectives are your friends in descriptive language, helping you bring life to your words.

Essay – The essay is also known as the Personal Statement in the context of college admissions. This is a written document in response to a prompt. A college essay is typically 250 words to 650 words.

Euphemisms – Words or phrases that act as substitutions for the literal word. For example, "He kicked the bucket" or "He bit the dust," when you should say, "he died," or "he is deceased. See Colloquialisms, Euphemisms, and Slang, in Chapter 11, "Mistake No. 10" in *Top 10 Mistakes Students Make*.

Extracurricular Activities – Any activities, outside of the high school curriculum, that includes, but is not limited to, sports, music, on-campus clubs, leadership programs, fine arts, governance (student council,

Associated Student Body), volunteer or community service, and discipline-specific activities (internships, research, or competitions).

First Generation College Student — Although there are many definitions concerning "first generation college students," Quetzal Mama defines this demographic as students whose parents did not receive a 4-year college diploma. This definition excludes parents who attended a 2-year college and/or enrolled, but did not complete/graduate from a 4-year college. This definition includes students who may have older siblings who are currently college students and/or graduates, but they still belong to the first generation within their respective family to attend college.

First-Person Narrative — This is the narrative in which you will write your Personal Statement. It is referred to as the first person singular, and represents the point of view of the author, through words and phrases such as "I" and "we."

Ganas — This is an intangible, personal quality or "essence" that is characterized by resilience, persistence, grit, tenacity, vision, and "guts." See Chapter 8, "The *Ganas* Principle."

Ganas **Principle** — This is Quetzal Mama's key principle to "nail" the Personal Statement. It is the essential quality that is represented in the student's essay that conveys the spirit in which they accomplished their goals. See Chapter 8, "The *Ganas* Principle."

Historically Underrepresented or Minority Student — A student who belongs to a racial and ethnic population that is underrepresented in higher education, relative to their numbers in the general population.

Specifically, we are referring to Latinos, African Americans, Native Americans (American Indians, Alaska Natives, and Native Hawaiians), Pacific Islanders, and mainland Puerto Ricans.

Honing the Senses — This is an effective way to engage the reader by providing vivid, sensory details. This allows the reader to more closely interpret and imagine the writer's perspective and experience. Honing the senses involves invoking one or more of the five senses: sight, smell, sound, taste, and touch.

Indirect Question — This is the unstated, implied question within a prompt. Identifying the indirect question requires the student to ask, "What is this prompt *really* asking of me?" See Chapter 4, "*Los Huesos —* The Bones."

Irony Punctuation — This is a rhetorical device used to denote the improper usage of a slang term by employing quotation marks. The quotation marks signify to the reader that you are intentionally misusing a slang term to convey irony or sarcasm. For example, "His professor accused him of using the 'race card' to accentuate his point." See Colloquialisms, Euphemisms, and Slang, in Chapter 11, "Mistake No. 10" in *Top 10 Mistakes Students Make*.

Ivy League — This term refers to the eight private colleges with the highest selectivity level for admission. The eight Ivy League schools include Brown University, Columbia University, Cornell University, Dartmouth College, Harvard University, Princeton University, the University of Pennsylvania, and Yale University.

Glossary

Los Huesos – Translated, this phrase means "The Bones." This is a Quetzal Mama writing strategy designed to help students identify and construct the fundamental structural components of an essay. This technique requires the writer to carefully analyze the prompt and identify both the direct and indirect questions asked. By answering the questions succinctly, the writer creates the "bones" or structure of their essay. See Chapter 4, *Los Huesos*: The Bones.

Narrative – Narrative can be defined in several ways, depending on the context. In the context of the Personal Statement we are speaking of the tense, form, or mode in which the author speaks. It is the grammatical first-person.

"Oh, incidentally" Strategy – This is a clever way to interweave student accomplishments into a Personal Statement without sounding conceited or boring. It requires students to "incidentally" include a personal fact or accomplishment within their Personal Statement. The key to this strategy is to create language that flows naturally, fluidly, and effortlessly. See Chapter 12, "*Essays Gone Wrong!*"

Personal Statement – This is an essay, written in response to a prompt, and required by most selective colleges and universities. The Personal Statement is typically 500 to 650 words.

Plagiarism – This is (a) using another person's words or ideas without properly citing your source(s); and (b) taking another person's work and attempting to pass it off as your own. See Chapter 3, "Getting Started – the Logistics."

Prompt – This term refers to a statement or question a student will respond to in essay format.

Reader Panel – A hand-picked team of individuals who will read and critique your Personal Statement. These members include, but are not limited to, an AP or IB English teacher, a community college English instructor, a university English professor, a local business person, or your school counselor. See Chapter 3, "*Getting Started – the Logistics.*"

Re-Purposing – also known as "Recycling." Re-Purposing is attempting to recycle a previously written Personal Statement by editing or modifying the content so that it can be *re-used* in response to a different prompt. See Chapter 3, "Getting Started – the Logistics."

Research 1 Institution – A designation assigned to a U.S. public or private university involved in extensive research that confers both undergraduate and graduate degrees (Master's & Doctoral).

SAT – The Scholastic Aptitude Test (SAT) is an exam administered by the College Board, testing critical reading, writing, and math. This exam is used for admission consideration at public and private universities.

Selective University: This term denotes top tier colleges in the United States. This term is synonymous with the rankings within the 2011 Barron's Guide to the Most Competitive Colleges, including the terms Most Competitive, Highly Competitive, and Very Competitive Plus categories. In general, selective colleges typically admit 10% to 20% of student applicants, with selectivity criteria especially stringent (90% percentile) for standardized tests and class ranking.

Slang — Informal words or phrases that may be inappropriate, lewd, or vulgar. See Colloquialisms, Euphemisms, and Slang, in Chapter 11, "Mistake No. 10" in *Top 10 Mistakes Students Make*.

Stream of Consciousness — This is a literary style in which the author's thoughts, feelings, and reactions are written (real-time) in a continuous flow. The writing represents the continuous flow of ideas and images as they occur to the writer, and are typically devoid of objective or conventional dialogue.

Taco de Carne Asada — This is a Quetzal Mama writing strategy designed to help students build their essay. The Personal Statement as a *Taco de Carne Asada* contains four elements. First, a corn tortilla or "shell" containing the introductory paragraph. Second, the *carne asada*, or the meat of the essay, providing the proof or examples of what is claimed in the introductory paragraph. Third, *el sabór*, or the flavor that comes from special additions or "flair" used for effect including the use of rhetorical devices, narrative style, tone, or a combination of several literary tools. Finally, the conclusion or finishing touch of our taco, where we close out the essay with a positive, impactful statement. See Chapter 6.

TIN CASA — This is a Quetzal Mama mnemonic tool that functions as a rubric to help students "check" themselves after drafting an essay. The acronym stands for Tone, Intellect, Narrative, Compelling (Introduction), Authenticity (Cultural), Speak (to audience), and Answer (the Question). See Chapter 7.

30527593R00141

Made in the USA
San Bernardino, CA
16 February 2016